THE
MEDITATION
— KIT —

THE
MEDITATION
KIT

Everything you need to relax and rejuvenate

CHARLA DEVEREUX and Fran Stockel

Illustrations by Rosamund Fowler

JOURNEY EDITIONS
BOSTON • TOKYO

This book is dedicated to the memory of Dorothy

ADVICE TO THE READER

Meditation is a useful aid to daily life, however it is not a substitute for normal personal healthcare and prompt medical attention where necessary. The adoption and application of the material offered in this kit is at the reader's discretion and sole responsibility. The author, packager and publisher cannot be held responsible in any manner whatsoever for any injury that may occur indirectly or directly from the use of this kit. If you are pregnant or suffer from any health problems or special conditions, or are in any doubt, please consult your doctor before using essential oils.

First published in 1997 by Journey Editions, an imprint of Tuttle Publishing, with editorial offices at 153 Milk Street, Boston, Massachusetts 02109.

Library of Congress Cataloging-in-Publication Data
Devereux, Charla, 1948–
    The meditation kit : the complete pack for meditation and
visualization / Charla Devereux and Fran Stockel.
        p. cm.
    Includes bibliographical references and index.
    ISBN 1-885203-48-9
    1. Meditation.   2. Visualization.   I. Stockel, Fran, 1930–   II. Title.
BF637.M4D48   1997
158.1`2—dc21   97–16729
                                                       CIP

Distributed by

Charles E. Tuttle Co., Inc.   Tuttle Shokai Ltd.
RR1 Box 231-5   1-21-13, Seki, Tama-ku,
North Clarendon, VT 05759   Kawasaki-shi 214, Japan
Tel: (800) 526-2778   Tel: (044) 833-0225
Fax: (800) FAX-TUTL   Fax: (044) 822-0413

First Edition
05 04 03 02 01 00 99 98 97   1 3 5 7 9 10 8 6 4 2

AN EDDISON•SADD EDITION
Edited, designed and produced by
Eddison Sadd Editions Limited
St Chad's House, 148 King's Cross Road
London WC1X 9DH

Phototypeset in Perpetua MT and Post Antiqua BE MT using QuarkXPress on Apple Macintosh
Printed by Dai Nippon Printing Company, Hong Kong
Packed by Hung Hing, China

CONTENTS

WHAT IS MEDITATION?

The gift of learning to meditate is the greatest gift you can give yourself in this life.
For it is only through meditation that you can
undertake the journey to discover your true nature, and to find the stability and
confidence you will need to live, and die, well.

SOGYAL RINPOCHE

Meditation is an ancient practice and a fundamental part of many traditional religions. Today, it is regarded as particularly helpful for reducing the stress and tension that so often prevail as a direct result of our busy lifestyle. More recently, people have turned to meditation for the specific purpose of improving their health and general well-being. Main-stream sectors of our culture are taking meditation practice seriously because there is a growing body of scientific evidence to back up the ancient wisdom. In view of its growing popularity, people are understandably seeking to learn how they may benefit from meditation and how to go about practising it. As they do, they will find that meditation is also a key which can open a door to inner spiritual realms (or at least to greater sensitivity and understanding) – a door which is currently closed to most Western minds, yet is there nonetheless, patiently waiting to be unlocked by meditation.

Newcomers to meditation, finding it an unfamiliar approach to solving their health or mental problems, often tend to make only sporadic or half-hearted attempts to meditate, and consequently do not experience any beneficial effects. As a result, they become disillusioned and give up. This is partly due to the realization that there is more than one way to go about the practice.

The Meditation Kit is specifically designed to help the beginner to avoid such pitfalls by providing a broad spectrum of guidance, helpful tools, and useful and important tips for those who have only a rudimentary understanding of meditation.

HOW DOES MEDITATION WORK?

The first principle of meditation is to be able to narrow attention to a manageable level. The aim is to free consciousness from the constraints of physiological need as well as from the usually overriding control of the logical conscious mind – in other words, to alter consciousness by 'switching off' the busy, chattering everyday mental mode that so dominates our waking lives.

There are many techniques that can be employed to help achieve the meditative state, and a number of Western approaches are explored in this book. The Appendix provides a brief but comprehensive description of the ancient traditions from which the modern concept of meditation comes, and readers are urged to become acquainted with this rich and important heritage. (All too often, people want to do things before they understand their history and nature.)

Meditation is achieved by focusing either on an object external to the body, a function of the body itself – such as breathing, or else on a single idea or thought. This may sound simple, but as many of us know only too well, it can prove difficult to focus single-mindedly on one mental target: our undisciplined habits of mind are hard to break. The means of meditation covered in this kit include the use of visual aids, auditory tools such as *mantras* (repetitive sounds of powerful resonance), breathing rhythms, and techniques using other senses such as smell and touch.

WHY MEDITATE?

In Eastern philosophies, the purpose of meditation is to reach nirvana (the original Hindu term for god-consciousness, later appropriated by Buddhism). Only the greatest teachers have been able to achieve and maintain this state of never-ending bliss. For most people, to open their heart in a truly unselfish way is a great beginning.

Through meditation, a state of equilibrium, perfect mental health, tranquillity and the ability to really see, to really hear and to be really present, are among potential benefits.

Meditation tends to alter the way your own existence is experienced. Although semantics and conceptualisations used in different schools and traditions of meditation may vary, the aim remains the same – to lead body and mind to the highest states of sensitivity and understanding of which a person is capable. Meditation is the path toward the unlimited potential of human experience.

A state of occasional bliss can sometimes be reached by an average meditator, and in some cases even nirvana can be attained for a short period of time. The memory of such an experience can live in the heart for ever and help keep the balance, especially during those turbulent periods which life surely brings to everyone from time to time.

WHAT MEDITATION DOES FOR YOU

Although meditation is not a substitute for medical intervention, it is increasingly recognized today as a useful tool for helping to reduce stress, which so readily results from modern lifestyles and can cause both mental and physical illnesses. For example, meditation helps relax insomniacs enough for them to enjoy a restful night's sleep. It can also be used to lower the anxiety level of people facing a serious operation, or to reduce tension caused by the anticipation of any potential stressful situation.

Whichever usage you want to make of meditation, physical well-being or spiritual experience (or both), it can bring positive and beneficial improvements to your present condition.

HOW THIS BOOK HELPS

The Meditation Kit is an ideal pack to give you everything you need to practise meditation successfully in your daily life. The book is fully comprehensive, giving useful background information on this ancient art as well as practical advice on how to do it. The first four chapters make up the practical 'how to' section of the book, and explain how the contents of the kit are used in meditation practice.

Chapter One provides general guidelines on how to prepare yourself and your environment and offers useful beginner's tips to help make your meditation successful. Chapter Two introduces and fully explores theme meditation, a concept which was specifically designed for this book. Meditating on a theme provides the beginner with an easily learned and effective method for the practice of meditation. Theme meditation also gives both the beginner and the more advanced meditator a meaningful focus, flexible enough to meet the specific needs of the individual. Chapter Three explores single-point meditation techniques including the use of visualization, as well as providing a selection of guided meditations. Chapter Four focuses on our senses of hearing, smell and touch, while suggesting a number of sensual aids that can be readily used.

In the latter part of this book, Chapter Five provides a brief survey of the medical benefits resulting from the practice of meditation that science is beginning to discover, and discusses some of the latest information available on meditation (including neurophysiological data). The Appendix covers the evolution of meditation through the centuries. It provides information on how meditation practices were used in earlier times, and how much of the wisdom learned from earlier traditions are being applied to our Western way of life. Those not aware of the history of meditation will thereby gain an appreciation and context for its practice.

As the benefits of meditation become increasingly discussed in the media, more and more people want to try it out as a way of promoting their health and well-being, and of coping with the stress of everyday life. This kit will be of great value to them, as well as to those already convinced by the idea of meditation as a beneficial method but who do not actually know how to set about practising it.

CONTENTS OF THE KIT

In order for the meditation to be as effective as possible, four meditational themes have been selected for this kit: Love, Peace, Balance and Transformation.

While the idea of focusing on a single thought is not new, the technique of theme meditation, along with its corresponding elements, is not only aiming to assist the beginner, but also to provide a fresh approach for those who already have some experience of meditation.

Each of the four themes has a corresponding image card which acts as a visual focus for the meditation.

The specially engineered audiotape contains a combination of mantras and natural sounds which also tie in to each of the four different themes.

The candle provided in the kit is used as a steady light source in 'point' meditation.

Full instructions are included on how to use all the different components as part of your meditation practice.

MEDITATION AND YOU

Once you have practised some, or all, of these techniques, you will feel comfortable using any of them at virtually any time – whenever you feel the need. A number of hints are provided to enable you to do just that.

The meditative experience will be different for each individual, but the essential aim is the same. Through the practice of meditation, much of what may seem like daily confusion can actually be transmuted into a more harmonious internal reality. Meditation can make it possible to sometimes say to yourself, 'It's okay,' and really mean it!

The goal of meditation, then, can be summarized as self-realization. In theory, if practised successfully and on a sufficiently large scale, meditation would actually be capable of bringing an end to much human suffering. This is an ambitious claim, but not an idle one.

Read on and practise some of the techniques discussed in this book so you can judge the wealth of benefits for yourself!

CHAPTER ONE

HOW TO START MEDITATING

*My mind withdrew its thoughts from experience,
extracting itself from the contradictory throng
of sensuous images, that it might find out
what that light was wherein it was bathed...*

ST AUGUSTINE

There are a number of ways in which meditation can be useful. For some people, the reason for deciding to try meditation can be as uncomplicated as just wanting to be able to relax. For others, the reason might be to assist them in their spiritual quest.

Various meditation techniques are discussed in this book, which are suitable for beginners and more experienced meditators alike. They all have the same basic objectives, so which you choose is strictly a question of personal preference. The main thing is to work with a technique that you feel most comfortable with.

Whatever meditation technique you choose, however, the first step is to prepare your meditational environment.

PREPARING FOR MEDITATION

In order to maximize the many beneficial effects that can be obtained from meditation, some commonsense tips are provided for preparing the mind, body and environment. Although initially it may seem that there is much to think about before you actually start meditating, with time you will begin to realize the wisdom of proper preparation, which will indeed become second nature to you. Preparation is a fundamental part of any process or ritual.

PLACE

Find a quiet place where you will not be disturbed and, preferably (though it is not absolutely necessary), one that you can use regularly for the purpose of meditation. If there are other people in the house, be sure to let them know that you do not want to be disturbed. It is best to turn off the phone if it is nearby; in the same way, turn off any answering machine, as a voice message coming through will be distracting.

Some people are lucky enough to have a large home in which an entire room can be devoted exclusively to relaxing pursuits, such as reading or meditating.

It is surprising how quickly a pleasant, calming atmosphere can build up in a chosen spot, and how it acts as a preparatory signal for meditation. On entering that space, even if you are unaware of its use, you are likely to feel a quality about it that is almost tangibly different from every other part of the home.

It is a sort of energy, very similar to that felt on entering a holy place of worship that has been used for very many years.

The atmosphere will reflect the energy produced by your meditation: this energy will build up and, eventually, those sensitive enough will walk into the room and feel it wash over them like waves of peace and comfort. Indeed, your own sensitivity to it will most likely increase as a result of continual meditation.

LIGHTING

It is best to have subdued lighting, if any is needed at all. If you choose to meditate during the day, be sure that the blinds or curtains are suitably drawn to prevent any glaring sunlight shining through the window for the next half-hour or so – particularly on to where you are sitting

Candlelight is the best kind of lighting for an otherwise dark room. If a candle is not available, then a low-wattage light bulb or low setting on the dimmer-switch is best. Or you may prefer no lighting in the room at all, with just the hint of a light coming from the hall or an adjoining room.

Soft lighting is preferable – aside from the peaceful ambience it provides – because a bright light could alter the state of consciousness you have already reached if your eyes were to open – for whatever reason – during your meditation.

TEMPERATURE AND CLOTHING

Make sure that, during meditation, you feel yourself to be in a warm, moderate temperature. This might mean a change of clothing. Whatever you do choose to wear, it ought to be loose-fitting, so that you are as comfortable and as unrestricted as possible (this is even more the case if you are planning to sit on the floor, in yoga posture). For the same reason, it is strongly recommended not to wear shoes while meditating. Barefoot is best, though thick socks are fine if the environment is cool.

It is worth remembering that body temperature usually falls slightly during meditation. This is a normal reaction, so you need not worry. In fact, it can serve as a guide to help you determine how deep your meditation actually was.

DIET

Your physiological state will play a part in the quality of your meditation. For instance, it is best not to meditate too soon after eating a major meal. And although it is not necessary to have fasted beforehand either, it is the case that a controlled fast can be a powerful aid in suitably altering the mind state for meditative purposes. It has been suggested by Richard J. Castillo, of the University of Hawaii, that fasting acts as a physiological aid – producing a state conducive to the focusing of attention. Fasting is often practised by yogis prior to meditation.

A sensible diet, however, with the emphasis on fresh fruits, vegetables and carbohydrates (not the sugary kind) rather than heavy protein and fats, is probably the most appropriate one to aid your meditational efforts. Try to avoid stimulants before meditation such as coffee, tea, cocoa, or soft drinks containing caffeine, or any particularly sugary food. If you want to drink something , a glass of water or orange juice would be best. It is well-known, at least at the folk level of direct experience, that what happens in the stomach can affect what happens in the head! An unquiet digestive system leads to an unquiet mind. When at ease and functioning well, the stomach and the rest of the digestive system provide the optimum bodily environment for the functioning of the brain and the reduction of stress.

Certain foods can actually dull the functioning of the mind, while others can enhance its effectiveness. For instance, essential fatty acids (vitamin F), which can only be obtained from food sources, are vital for the health of cell membranes, nerve fibres and brain cells among other things. These are found in oily fish such as cod, mackerel, herring and salmon, as well as in vegetable oils. The salmon of wisdom, indeed! There is much research to be done on this overlooked aspect of consciousness study, but for here and now, self-experimentation is called for, along the lines given here. What you eat really can affect how you mentally function.

TIMING

There is no particular time in the day when it is best to meditate; nor do you need to set any particular limit to the amount of time you spend on each meditation. However, timing is an important element in ensuring a successful meditation. Here are a few guidelines that will help you to choose or decide.

WHEN IS THE BEST TIME TO MEDITATE?
Inevitably, for most people, available time is determined by events such as work schedules and family commitments, so that rather than being able to choose a time, it is more or less chosen for you!

You may prefer to set aside time in the evening, to help you get over the stresses of the day: meditation in the evening can be very helpful in encouraging a good night's sleep.

Alternatively, you may want to start your day with a meditation, to be able to cope more easily with what the day may have in store. Ideally, if you are fortunate enough, you may find the time to meditate twice a day.

Meditating at the same time every day can be helpful. Your mind will adapt more readily to the meditative state, and entering it will become easier: in effect, you are programming yourself to meditate at that particular time. It is important, however, not to force a meditation should it not feel appropriate, even though it may be at the time you have set aside for it.

Whatever time of the day you choose, it is best not to have any pressing commitments directly afterwards, so that you need not worry about having to set yourself a time limit.

HOW LONG SHOULD MEDITATION LAST?
The amount of time you spend on your standard daily meditation is determined by the type of meditation you choose to do – that is to say, what you want to achieve by meditating.

Meditation can last anywhere from 20 minutes to one hour. In Western practice, about 15 minutes are considered necessary to empty and settle the mind; and 10 or 15 minutes to enter into the actual meditative state. (Of course, people who are engaged in deep spiritual meditation can remain in that state for an indeterminate amount of time.)

At the end of your meditation, another 20 minutes or so should ideally be allowed to emerge from the state, and to quietly absorb and reflect upon what has just been experienced. If you have to go to work after meditating, this will provide your body and your mind with a smooth transition period to return to 'normal' consciousness. Also, you may enjoy extending the peaceful atmosphere that the meditation is likely to have created.

When you need to set a specific time limit, then arrange things carefully. For example, the use of a timer can cause a severe jolt, particularly if you are in a deep state when it goes off. One suggestion is that you bury an alarm clock under a pillow or two, to muffle the sound when it rings, or that you place it in another room. The best option would be to set up a gently chiming clock in another room.

Do not feel pressured if, for whatever reason, you are not able to meditate in specific allotments of time. These are only guidelines. You will need to establish what is best and most suitable for your own personal needs. For instance, beginners often find that even 10 minutes is too long at first. This will be particularly true for people who are very tense and have never experienced any relaxation exercises: as the body relaxes, it releases tension in a variety of ways which, to the beginner, may feel strange and even uncomfortable.

BODY RHYTHMS

Just like the ocean cycle of tides, the body has its own daily rhythms — which can often determine our daily actions, or at least guide us as to what are the best moments for performing certain activities – such as meditation.

Some of those rhythms are easily observed — such as the time of day when hunger sets in, or when energy is at a low point. Other changes that occur, for instance small shifts in body temperature, are less obvious; yet body temperature does change throughout the day in accord with its own cycle — usually from a low point in the early morning to a high point in the afternoon. This temperature change happens to almost everyone who sleeps at night and is active during the day.

Most functions of the body are subject to daily rhythms — including blood sugar levels, kidney functions and brain chemistry. Have you ever noticed, for example, that when your head or nose is affected by a cold it feels better in the morning than it does at night? These types of cyclical changes in our adrenal hormone level can affect the way we react to stress. Our hormone level, like other functions of the body, follows its own pattern of highs and lows, sometimes linked to external cycles such as light and darkness.

Meditation provides us with an opportunity to tune into these internal body rhythms, and to become more conscious of them. At first, actually listening to your own heartbeat might be disturbing. Once you get used to it, however, you will find that listening to your own body rhythm while in a relaxed state is a very pleasant experience which can actually deepen the level of relaxation.

If you are able to practise your meditation twice a day, even for a little while – such as when you are on holiday – try to see if you can notice an overall difference after about a week. For some people, morning meditation can be like a tonic which energizes them for the day. On the other hand, after an evening meditation they may have a soothing, but almost lethargic, reaction.

POSTURE

Choose a spot where you feel most comfortable. A straight-backed chair is recommended. If you use a well-worn sofa or a soft armchair, prop yourself up with a few firm pillows. You may prefer sitting on the floor, but unless you are used to it, you may find yourself fidgeting and focusing on the ache in your back instead of your meditation point.

If sitting on a seat, do not cross your legs; keep your feet apart and flat on the floor. Your hands should rest comfortably so as not to be distractive. Place them close to your knees or in your lap, palms up or palms down You may prefer to keep them separate, or hold one hand cupped in the other.

If you feel it is important to be on the floor, stools designed especially for meditating can be purchased: the seat slopes forward, allowing your legs to be tucked underneath it so that you are basically kneeling on the floor, while the weight of your body does not fall on your heels. Sitting on the floor is generally associated with positions taught in yoga. The three following *asanas* (body postures) shown provide a small sample of how concentration, when focused on the body, can affect physical well-being. Any one of them can be incorporated into your own meditation.

With hands resting on or close to the knees, hold thumb and forefingers curved with joining tips.

Or you may prefer to hold your hands cupped in your lap, with one hand resting in the other.

The stool seat slopes forward, allowing your legs to be tucked comfortably underneath it, so that you are kneeling on the floor with your buttocks resting on the stool.

SUKHASANA (THE EASY POSE)

This is the easiest of all of the asana postures, consisting of sitting cross-legged on the floor. First, sit on the edge of a small, low cushion. Once you are comfortable, stretch your legs straight out in front of you. Slowly bend the left leg towards your body, and tuck the left foot under the right leg, beneath the thigh. Now do the same with the right leg: bend it towards the body, and position it under the left leg.

This posture allows the body to be held erect. Your hands should be spread loosely, palms facing up and resting gently on or close to the knees, thumb and forefingers curved into a circle with the tips joining (this finger position is optional). Or you may prefer to rest your hands with the palms facing down on the knees.

Stop when you start to feel any discomfort: you will find that you need some time to build up to being able to maintain the posture for longer periods.

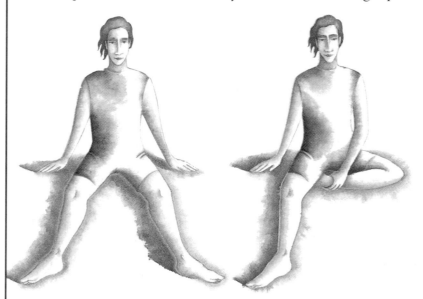

1. Sit on the edge of a small, low cushion and stretch your legs straight out in front of you.

2. Pull the left leg towards your body, and tuck the left foot under the right leg, beneath the thigh.

3. Pull the right leg towards the body and position it under the left leg so that you are comfortable. Rest your hands on your knees with thumb and forefinger touching at the tips; or with palms facing down.

PADMASANA (THE LOTUS POSE)

Of all the yoga postures, padmasana is probably the most familiar to the West. It is called the lotus pose because the position of the feet resembles lotus petals. Although this pose is often found to be difficult if not physically impossible to attain, it is offered here for those who wish – and are able – to use it as part of their meditation practice.

Padmasana is more easily acquired by people with supple limbs; it may take longer for those who have taken up yoga postures at a later age.

Sit on a small cushion on the floor, close to the edge (this gives support to your spine). Extend your legs forward. Take hold of your left foot with both hands and place it on your right thigh, with the sole of the foot turned upwards. Now take your right foot and bring it up over the left leg, so that it can be similarly placed on the left thigh. (At first, you may find it difficult to get the right leg over the left leg.) After you have used it for a while, you may well discover a new supple condition of limbs, body and mind.

2. Place your left foot on your right thigh, with the sole of the foot turned upwards.

1. Sit on a small cushion on the floor, legs apart stretched out in front of you.

3. Take hold of your right foot with both hands and bring it up to rest on your left thigh, sole turned upwards. Rest your hands on your knees with thumb and forefinger touching at the tips.

SIDDHASANA (THE POSE OF PERFECTION)

This pose was often used by mystics, who were thought to be perfect – hence its name: The Pose of Perfection.

Start by sitting on the floor, again using a small cushion.

Extend both legs straight out in front of you.

Take your left foot with your right hand and gently draw it towards the body, so that the left heel can be placed directly beneath you, with the sole of the left foot touching the right thigh. The left leg must be completely doubled in order to acquire this posture. Then bring your right leg over, so that it is also doubled, with your foot resting above the left ankle, and your toes resting gently between the calf and thigh of your left leg.

The body will be kept erect. Choose any of the hand positions described in the sukhasana *(see page 17)*. Make sure it is comfortable so that you are not distracted.

This pose does require constant practice, but do not be discouraged: it can be attained.

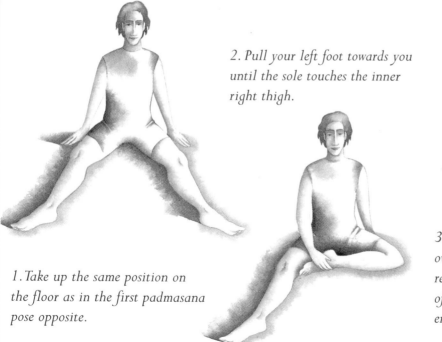

2. Pull your left foot towards you until the sole touches the inner right thigh.

1. Take up the same position on the floor as in the first padmasana pose opposite.

3. Now bring your right foot to lie over your left ankle, with the toes resting between the calf and thigh of the left leg. Keep your body erect throughout this asana.

Whether you decide to sit on a seat or on the floor, remember to keep your spine as erect as possible in order to achieve a good balance of relaxation and alertness.

Sitting is preferable to lying down, as a prone posture may well induce sleep, particularly if you are not a seasoned meditator.

Once you have found a position that suits you, it is best to use it every time you meditate. Your body will become used to that particular posture, and your mind will also associate it with meditation.

This does not mean that you cannot experiment with other postures; but it is a good idea to decide on one basic position that you can associate with your usual meditation time.

If at any time during your meditation you begin to feel a little uncomfortable from sitting in the same position, do not hesitate to shift and change it slightly. The important thing to remember is that you will experience a better meditation if you are comfortable.

Trying to remain perfectly still, while feeling a nagging discomfort in your back or neck, will only cause you to lose concentration and detract from the meditative process. Master yogis may have to learn to overcome all discomfort, but we can allow ourselves more flexibility!

BREATHING TECHNIQUES

After completing initial preparation, the next step is to fully relax the body before starting any form of meditation. This is what breathing techniques are designed to do.

Breathing can be a powerful tool for meditation, and many traditional meditational systems use breathing techniques to regulate the breathing pattern, which in turn helps to calm the mind. When breath is controlled by esoteric methods, not only does it help to attain a state of altered consciousness, it can also bring about a whole physical regenerative process.

Few people walk or sit properly, or, more importantly, breathe properly – leading to types of illnesses likely to be alleviated solely by the proper control of the breath. The yogis and other highly trained spiritual teachers have tried to share with us some of the essential knowledge needed to attain the state of altered consciousness reached in meditation.

The first and essential lesson to remember is to always breathe through the nose. Nasal breathing filters out many of the dangerous elements or impurities in the air, thereby making use of the full system nature gave us.

When we breathe through the mouth, we not only short-cut that system, but we also allow impurities to enter our system freely.

In addition to being a protective filter, the nose also serves to warm the air that is inhaled to a suitable temperature before it enters the body. Inflammation of the respiratory organs often results from breathing in cold air through the mouth. After all, you would not fly off into outer space without being in a suitable vehicle: similarly, do not try to voyage into inner space without taking the same care.

SWAR YOGA

Swar yoga (unification through breath) took breathing a step further by identifying the best moments of the day for meditation, namely when the individual is breathing predominantly through the left nostril.

It may surprise you to realize that one nostril is normally dominant over the other when you breathe, and, more amazing, that this dominance switches approximately every hour.

Neurophysiologists have learnt that the right hemisphere of the brain — which causes a person to be passive and introverted — controls the left side of the body, while the left hemisphere of the brain controls the right side of the body.

According to yogic belief, the left nostril affects the right hemisphere of the brain; therefore it is the preferred nostril to be dominant during the meditative process.

When the right nostril dominates, the individual is likely to be distracted, or restless. Fortunately, nostril dominance can be easily altered by lying down on the opposite side of the body. It only takes a few minutes for gravity to drain the sinuses and produce the desired result.

YOGA PRANA

Yogis are able to direct their breath to any part of the body they choose, usually with amazing physical results. They tell us that when we inhale and exhale a combination of oxygen, hydrogen and nitrogen, we also breathe in something called *prana*. This is a Sanskrit term which means 'absolute energy'. Yogis believe that prana is necessary for every thought and motion. It is found in all living things, and is considered to be the active principle or vitality of life itself. This is why yogis feel that proper breathing is so important — it provides a constant supply of prana.

Whether or not this image is literally true, it is unfortunately the case for most of us that in our daily life we are not receiving all the oxygen our body can utilize.

In meditation, deep breathing floods the body with the extra energy needed — an oxygen surplus which helps to still and calm the mind. (According to folk wisdom, when you feel frustrated or irritated, all you need to do is to take in several slow, deep breaths, and you will feel almost instant relief.)

It is important to keep an even rhythm between inhalation and exhalation, so as to maintain a balance. One very basic breathing technique is to inhale slowly and fully, while visualizing the air as it enters your nose and fills your body — just like water filling a vessel, or light making your body resplendent. The exhalation should be a smooth, gentle release of the breath: a gentle, wave-like rhythm, like the ebb and flow of the sea.

YOGA COMPLETE BREATH

Many yoga practices teach this technique, designed to exercise all parts of the respiratory tract and lungs. It consists of three basic steps:

1. Sit erect and breathe in through the nostrils, first filling the lower part of the lungs, then the middle, and finally the top part. This should be done in one, slow, steady breath.

2. Hold the breath for a few seconds.

3. Exhale slowly, holding the chest in a firm position and drawing in the abdomen a little. Lift the chest upwards slowly as the air leaves the lungs. Once the air is exhaled both chest and abdomen can be relaxed.

YOGA CLEANSING BREATH

This is another valuable yoga breathing technique, and is a good practice to use at the end of your meditation.

When you have completed your meditation, make sure you allow yourself time to gradually return to waking consciousness. In this way, the tranquillity that you will have experienced can be carried over into your daily life, rather than being abruptly cut off.

You may even want to include a few simple stretching exercises before setting about your normal routine.

1. Inhale deeply.

2. Hold the air a few seconds.

3. Pucker the mouth and exhale some of the air vigorously through the lips.

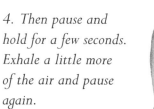

4. Then pause and hold for a few seconds. Exhale a little more of the air and pause again.

5. Repeat steps 3 and 4 until all of the air has been exhaled.

COUNTING TECHNIQUE

One very simple breathing technique is to sit motionless, breathe slowly and count the breaths from one to ten. When you reach ten, start again with one, and continue in this manner. This sounds almost too easy, but you will soon discover how difficult it is to concentrate on even a basic body function such as this. Your thoughts distract you, your attention wanders, and you are left sitting there facing your undisciplined mental activity.

Do not be discouraged, however; with practice, conscious breathing can quite quickly calm and order the usual shambles of the mental processes. It is crucial to appreciate that the way we breathe can have a direct bearing on the quality of our meditation.

PULSE COUNT

Another way to control the breath is by counting the pulse. Yogis often synchronize their rhythmic breathing with the beat of their heart. You can too, thereby establishing your own personal rhythm. (Obviously this type of breathing cannot be practised in group meditation because each person is likely to have a different rhythm.)

To make it work best, place your fingers on your pulse and count the beats as you breathe, until the rhythm becomes firmly fixed in your mind. On average, it usually takes about six counts or pulse units to fully inhale – but count up to whatever number is comfortable for you. When you have fully inhaled, hold your breath for a few counts, then gently exhale using the same number of counts as you did while inhaling. Continue this practice until you feel totally at ease, and your mind is quiet.

You may like to follow the yogic rule for rhythmic breathing, which says that the number count for inhalation and exhalation should be the same, while the count for retention and between breaths should be half that number.

PRANAYAMA

An important aspect of using breath in meditation (pranayama) is to become conscious of which nostril is the passage for air *(see Swar yoga page 21)*, as the left-right interaction can have a bearing on the binary systems of the brain and thus the mode of consciousness.

Using your pulse, breathe in through the left nostril for four beats, hold the breath eight beats and breathe out for four beats through the right nostril. Repeat this using the alternating nostrils. It is alright to close the unused nostril with light pressure from your finger. Maintain this alternating rhythmic breathing for as long as you feel comfortable; it may be a little confusing at first, but allow yourself time to settle into a rhythm.

In kundalini yoga, you alternate the right and left paths of energy, symbolized respectively as solar and lunar currents which criss-cross up the spine and meet in the 'third eye', as in the caduceus of Mercury. By using your nostrils in this breathing exercise, you are attempting to activate spinal, kundalini energy.

A WORD OF ADVICE

A number of unexpected body reactions can occur during meditation, which could cause some concern unless you are given due warning.

Meditational side effects or discomforting sensations are sometimes experienced as a result of deep relaxation. These side effects usually disappear within only a matter of minutes. Depending on how 'wound-up' you are prior to commencing the meditation, you may experience sudden jolts or tremors as your body unwinds.

This is perfectly natural, and you may already be familiar with some of them, for they can also happen just before you fall asleep, particularly after a hectic day, perhaps accompanied by the sudden feeling that you are falling off a cliff – and this usually has the effect of immediately bringing you back into a fully awakened state.

When these body reactions or tension releases occur in meditation, it is usually during the beginning stages, just at the very point when you are starting to relax.

As the body is relaxing, other sensations, which may affect the whole body or only a part of it, include a feeling of heaviness – as if you were being drawn downwards – or, quite the opposite, a feeling of weightlessness – just as if gravity has suddenly been removed.

Specific sensations within the body, such as alteration of temperature, an itch, numbness, or tingling, can often be felt. Pulsations are some-times experienced in various other parts of the body – but especially on the top of the head.

Remember that these are all normal reactions. They can take place when you start to relax, and are usually connected to the amount of tension in the body at the onset of meditation.

The best way to deal with tension-releasing sensations such as these is to first acknowledge that they are normal, and then to continue meditating by bringing your attention back to the focus point of your meditation.

Some people have reported that, while they were meditating they experienced certain 'phantom' smells, tastes or sounds.

I remember how once, during meditation, I heard incredible music, and assumed that the radio had been on at its lowest sound level. What sounded to me like music from the celestial spheres soothingly filled my head for several minutes before I lost consciousness of it. After the meditation I went over to turn the radio off, only to discover to my amazement that it had not been on at all!

Whether these sensations are an amplification of the thought process or simply random events, they should always be treated as you would a stray thought entering your mind: take note of it, then let it float past, as if you were sitting in the sun beside a lovely stream and dreamily observing the gentle ripples created by the flow of the fresh and pure water.

PRINCIPLES OF THEME MEDITATION

At this point, you are ready to drift into a meditative state, or to use one of the meditative techniques discussed in this book.

It is not a good idea, however, especially for the beginner, to simply try to blank out the mind. It is much better to focus on an external or mental object, so as to bring the often chaotic actions of the mind to order.

Choose a theme

An exceptionally useful mental object, for beginners and Western practitioners in general, is a theme, because no effort need be spent on negating the processes of thought: only in bringing them into control and focus.

It is worth noting that, while the concept of theme meditation is new, and the method and tools have been especially designed for this kit, the principles of this type of meditation are based on traditional practice.

The four themes:
Love, Peace, Balance, Transformation

Four themes have been selected for *The Meditation Kit*, designed to offer as broad a meditational range as possible, as well as a variety of levels — sensory, intellectual, mental, symbolic and spiritual — on which to meditate.

The four meditational themes are: Love, Peace, Balance and Transformation.

Choosing which of these themes to work with will depend on your own, particular purpose for meditation.

How to use these themes for meditation is described in detail for you in the next chapter, 'Theme meditation'.

Focus on a word

One suggestion is to first focus only on the generic 'name', or concept, of the theme itself: in other words love, peace, balance or transformation, to explore what it means for you. Indeed, you may be surprised to realize that your initial definition of the word is rather limiting.

After having worked with the themes for a while, you will be able to explore for yourself the vast range of experience they have to offer.

Theme meditation

In the next chapter, you will learn how to practise theme meditation. The potential range of each theme is discussed, to help you choose the best one for your purpose.

Each theme has its own set of correspondences or aids, which includes an image card, a colour, a mantra and a sound, each representative of the particular theme.

All these aspects of a theme can be used in a number of ways which are fully explored in this book, to help enhance the quality of your meditation while also keeping you focused on the theme that you yourself have chosen.

MEDITATION TOOLS

To support your theme meditation, a number of useful aids are provided in this kit.

Four coloured cards represent the visual symbols – image and colour – of each of the four meditation themes. The related mantras and evocative ambient sounds of each theme are reproduced on an audiotape.

Utilizing both sight and sound, these meditational tools will provide valuable assistance in enhancing, focusing and helping to set the mental mood necessary for the meditation.

You will soon learn how to choose one to suit your personal quest; and how to use the relevant tools provided.

CHAPTER TWO

THEME MEDITATION

*…remember: a method is only a means, not the meditation itself.
It is through practising the method skilfully
that you reach the perfection of that pure state of total presence,
which is the real meditation.*

SOGYAL RINPOCHE

An excellent meditation technique is the use of a theme as a mental object to focus on. It is particularly helpful for beginners, because the mere fact of having to concentrate on a theme allows the normal thinking processes to commence moving towards what is the relatively unfamiliar meditative state.

The theme acts like a funnel that draws in our thinking from its usual scattered condition and moves it forward in an ever narrowing stream of concentration.

Furthermore, the themes chosen for this kit operate on several levels – intellectual, instinctual, symbolic and sensory. This multi-level organizing of our attention is an exceedingly effective way of marshalling our mental powers. This method acts as a psychic motor that propels us towards the meditation goal.

THE FOUR THEMES

Love, Peace, Balance and Transformation are the four themes selected for this kit. They were chosen because together they cover a broad range of experience. The theme of Love encompasses all matters of the heart and personal relationships. Peace ranges from universal harmony to your own spiritual centre. Balance covers current experience and life patterns. Transformation, as the name suggests, relates to changes in your life.

Each theme has its own associated colour, image card, mantra and background sound. Knowledge of these aspects of a theme will enable you to design your own meditation.

The kit provides useful aids to support your theme meditations. You will find four image cards illustrated in colour, as well as an audiotape which contains mantras and background sounds; these correspond with each of the four themes.

The cards and the tape can be used simultaneously or individually in a number of different ways, which will allow you to vary your meditative sessions. However, initially at least, choose to keep your meditation simple.

For now, please read through all the themes: it will give you a feeling of their range and content, and enable you to make a better personal choice for your meditation.

HOW TO USE THE MEDITATIONAL TOOLS

It is not necessary to use all the tools for each theme at once. To begin with it is best to use just one of the tools per meditation. As you become familiar with the principles of theme meditation, you may decide to try combining several techniques together, for example using the image card while listening to the tape.

Above all, it is important to remember that there is no 'correct' way to use the various tools provided in this kit. The uses for the tools are as varied as your imagination.

HOW TO CHOOSE A THEME

Your choice of a theme, or mental object, to focus on will be determined by your own personal situation and need to meditate.

For example, if you have just quarrelled with your best friend and are feeling rather alone, then the Love theme would be an apt choice. As you explore the meaning of love, either by focusing visually on the image card of the rose, or listening to the background sound of the bees – which can bring to mind a beautiful garden on a summer's day – the anger you felt towards your friend as a result of your quarrel seems to melt away.

Once the anger has subsided, it is easier to consider your friend's point of view. You may find that your differences are very much smaller than you initially thought.

On the other hand, you could use the meditational pathway provided by the Love theme when you are not in a state of argument with anybody, but when in fact you are feeling particularly harmonious and at one with the world! For the fundamental nature of love, which underlies its myriad manifestations, is oneness.

This experience of oneness is the ultimate goal of meditation on a theme. These two extreme examples, from the detailed and personal to the general and cosmic, show what a wide range of mental and emotional contexts a theme like this can serve. So it is with every powerful theme – the ones used in this book and others you may in time develop for yourself.

The theme of Peace would be a good choice if you are having to come to terms with a decision that has already been made, but with which you are not in total agreement. The same principles that apply to nations also apply on a smaller scale such as the relationship between you and those you may work with. Sometimes it is necessary to compromise, which means being willing to give something up no matter how important it may be to you. Meditating on the theme of peace can assist in the process.

This theme may also prove helpful in attaining levels of comfort at difficult periods in your life. In its deepest form, the Peace theme could even lead to profound mystical experience – the 'peace that passeth understanding'.

If you are having to decide between what appears to be two opposing forces, meditating on the theme of Balance could be useful. It can be helpful to weigh the potential benefits of each choice against each other until a centre point is reached. By working with this theme, you might even be able to discover a potential middle way which can often be a combination of some of the positive benefits of each side. Thus by finding the centre ground or balance point, what may have initially been perceived as being in opposition can be brought into harmony.

The Balance theme can also help to level out the warring forces within yourself. It is a wonderful theme to work with if you are experiencing a lot of unwanted stress in your life. Indeed, the Balance theme is a good one to work with to help reduce stress either mental or physical that you may be experiencing. So conditions of stress, whether caused on any level in mind, body or social interaction, can all be better handled by meditating on Balance.

You may be at the point of having to make a decision that could completely change the course of your present situation. In this case, Transformation would be a good mental object to work with. Many people are resistant to change because it often means stepping into an unknown situation, and so they will choose to stay with something that is familiar. Meditating on the Transformation theme can help prepare for those inevitable changes that occur in life for which no choice is provided.

The Transformation theme may also be useful when dealing with physical and emotional illness, because it can help you to understand the significance of the greater changes in life. These changes, or transformations, come in all shapes and sizes, from changes in job to changes in personal status (from being single to being married, for instance) changes in health, and ultimately, that most awesome and greatest of all changes we have to face, that of death itself.

MEDITATION AND CHAKRAS

From time to time in this book, there are references to 'chakras'. In Eastern tradition, the chakra system is an intricate network of invisible strands of energy which come together at specific junctures in the body. These junctures, or chakras, are where the physical and subtle bodies are said to meet.

There are seven major chakras, found along a shaft of the subtle body that is believed to be located within the spinal column. The seven major chakras are the crown, or *sahasrara*, situated just above the crown of the head, which relates to spirituality; the brow chakra, or *ajna*, situated at the centre of the brow between the two eyebrows, and often referred to as 'the third eye'; the throat, or *vishuddha*, the creative centre – especially of the spoken word; the heart, or *anahata*, associated with every kind of love; the solar plexus, or *manipura*, connected with emotion; the sacral chakra, or *swadisthana*, situated halfway between the navel and the pubis, said to open the intuitive and psychic powers; the base, or *muladhara*, located at the base of the spine and for this reason sometimes referred to as the root centre.

They are associated with meditation themes. For example, by concentrating on the heart chakra in the course of your meditation on the Love theme, you will increase your receptivity to emotion and feeling and enhance the quality of your feelings.

THE SEVEN MAJOR CHAKRAS

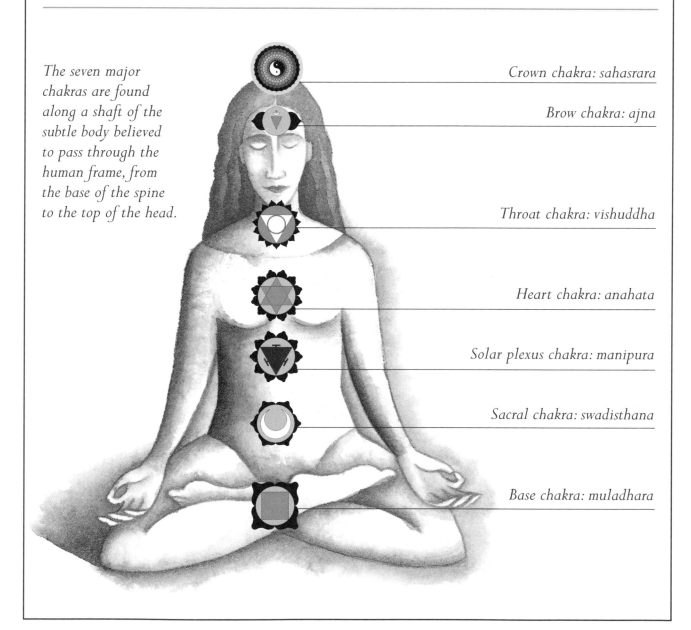

The seven major chakras are found along a shaft of the subtle body believed to pass through the human frame, from the base of the spine to the top of the head.

Crown chakra: sahasrara

Brow chakra: ajna

Throat chakra: vishuddha

Heart chakra: anahata

Solar plexus chakra: manipura

Sacral chakra: swadisthana

Base chakra: muladhara

LOVE

Use this theme for meditation on all matters of the heart and for personal relationship issues

- Pave the way for re-establishing a close relationship after a quarrel.
- Explore what the word 'love' means to you.
- Get in tune with your own potential, which allows you to learn to love yourself.
- Understand how you feel when you are 'in love'.
- Discover the meaning of cosmic or divine love.

PEACE

Use this theme for meditation to help attain comfort in any difficult period of your life

- Come to terms with an unwanted decision.
- Focus on universal harmony or world peace.
- Try to deal with a particularly uncomfortable situation.
- Get in touch with your spiritual centre.
- Overcome any personal feeling of guilt.
- Be generous to yourself by forgiving yourself at least as easily as you do others.

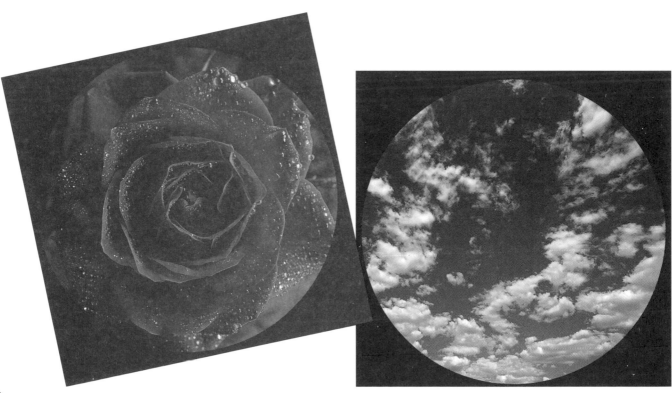

BALANCE

Use this theme for meditation on how you can weigh opposing forces in your life to achieve a middle way

- Establish an appropriate course of action from opposing viewpoints.
- Find the reasons for set patterns in your life.
- Explore the meaning of the term *maya* – the illusion of life.
- Discover how to swim with the tide, not against it.
- Focus on current experience – the centre point between past and present.

TRANSFORMATION

Use this theme for meditation on a need to make a decision that will result in a change in your life

- Deal with life-changing decisions that will affect your personal circumstances.
- Find comfort during times of transition – especially when unexpected.
- Explore the meaning of spirituality.
- Understand the cycle of life by becoming aware of its natural progression.
- Cope with death by casting a totally different light on it.

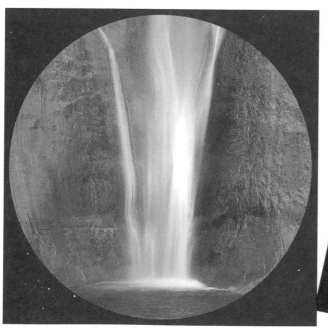

~ LOVE ~

*...the rose garden of temporal love is itself
but the mortal image of its immortal concept.*

BARBARA SEWARD

In everyday life, too many distractions, too many conditioned responses get in the way of achieving the 'free' state of love that is within our reach. In meditation, all distractions and worldly constraints are removed, giving the mind the chance to experience love in its unconditional, 'higher' state.

Meditation also helps to break down the layers of pre-programmed defensiveness, allowing for more openness and a greater ability to feel and express new dimensions of love. If you feel secure within yourself, it is easier to allow others to be what they really are. Game playing becomes less important.

WHAT IS LOVE?

Those of us brought up in a predominantly Western society acquire most of our concepts about love from outside ourselves. There is a continual bombardment of advertisements on television, in magazines, on billboards and so on, which reflects the current cultural concept of the ideal image. Then, of course, there is Hollywood, and all the glamour and glitz that comes with that package. All this makes a lot of people feel unworthy of what are, in fact, the most unrealistic concepts of love imaginable. Yet they accept what they are shown, and some try very hard to emulate it, even though deep down there is the knowledge that it is fantasy. Self-esteem is demoralized because, realistically, most of life can never fit the idealized fairy tale that is so often projected. So what can be done about this?

The first step is to understand that real love has absolutely nothing to do with these superficial projections. Love comes from within. The practice of meditation allows each individual to explore for him or herself what the meaning of love really is, and to realize that it needs no artificial outer trappings. Love is found in self-acceptance, non-judgment and joy. These are truly fulfilling spiritual aspirations, and they can be better understood by focusing on their meaning.

Meditation is an incredible tool which can help everyone to learn, to understand, and to accept themselves for who they are. Once this is achieved, they can truly love themselves, and therefore fully love others as well as opening up to being loved in return.

Pir Vilayat Inayat Khan, Sufi leader in the West, explained at one of his seminar weekends that when two people come together, there are usually four energies involved: those of the two fantasizing individuals, and those of the two real ones. At first, the woman projects all her needs and fantasies on to the unsuspecting male, then decides that he may actually be that projection. Simultaneously, the male is doing the same thing. Unfortunately, the real people can never be seen until all their projections and expectations are 'unrealized'. This is the point when anger, disappointment and frustrations enter the relationship. Until that stage, the two people have never really met, never really 'seen' each other.

Love between people is achieved when their emotional energies are comfortable within themselves, when respect, sensitivity, compassion and, most importantly, friendship for one another form the fundamental theme. In many relationships, one personality is totally dominant, and with the subservient partner accepting the role without question. Individuals must be free to be who they are. When this energy is curtailed, the soul withdraws and is diminished – the fire is taken away from the life force. Trees must have equal sunlight to grow. If one takes most of the light the other will die. So it is with human relationships.

Love is not just receiving, it is also giving. For love to find completion in human beings, it must extend into compassion. In its essence, it is a selfless force – universal rather than personal. The key is to avoid becoming possessive in any way, otherwise there is a risk of destroying what has been lovingly created. On the other hand, a selfless person can often be misunderstood, and be taken advantage of by those who are more ego-centred. Therefore be alert. If a relationship does not contain mutual respect it is best to let it go, because continuing can only ultimately bring pain.

DIVINE LOVE

Divine love is a totally different experience from human love; it requires spiritual development. Mystics soon find that the love they are really seeking is mystical union with what is known as the Divine Ground – the transcendental state of total grace.

No human seems capable of god-like love. Most of us feel that we are unworthy of such an attainment, but by using meditation to lift us beyond our mundane state of being we can, in fact, come to truly experience this heightened order of unconditional love.

In deep meditation, ecstasy greater than any sensual feeling can fill your entire being. This is what the mystics call cosmic love. It encompasses everything: all things, all beings, all worlds. In it you are lost, and at last you are released from the constraints of the self-centred ego.

Krishnamurti, the important spiritual teacher of the early twentieth century, has this to say about love: 'Do you know what it means to love somebody? Do you know what it means to love a tree, or a bird or a pet animal, so that you care for it, feed it, cherish it, though it may give you nothing in return? … Most of us don't love that way, we do not know what that means because all our love is always hedged with anxiety, jealousy and fear which implies that we depend inwardly on another. We want to be loved. We don't just love and leave it there, we ask something in return and in that very asking we become dependent. To love is not to ask anything in return, not even to feel you are giving something, and it is only such love that can know freedom.'

This state is attainable for every one of us. It is time to open up the channels that lead to it through meditation.

THE SYMBOL OF LOVE: THE ROSE

The rose is a universal symbol which has many representations, including perfection, beauty, birth and rebirth, motherhood and the heart, or centre, of life. It is the flower of goddesses, and when associated with the sun it depicts love, life and creation. In early times, roses were used in love philters (potions to make people fall in love). In alchemy, the rose symbolizes mystical or divine love. The mystical marriage, or union of opposites, takes place in the rose garden which itself is a symbol of paradise. Fairy tales of all nations and ages speak of the rose as the magic flower of love. It is the flower of early spring. For the Egyptians, the rose symbolized pure love, and served as an emblem for Aphrodite, the Greek goddess of love.

Symbolism was dominant in medieval and romantic literature: it was used by writers to express what might otherwise be inexpressable. For example, Dante used the rose to express paradise and divine love in *The Divine Comedy*. Aspects of nature were also used by the early romantics to symbolize human emotion and sentiment. The idea of the rose representing beauty and love was revived from the earlier secret esoteric teachings, and brought into mainstream consciousness.

Our modern twentieth-century writers often draw on the imagery from these times and so the rose has now become the symbol of all affirmative values, chief among these being love.

THE COLOUR OF LOVE: PINK/RED

The colour red, probably the most dynamic of all the colours, is traditionally associated with power, physical energy, strength and fire. It is the colour of blood, the expression of vital life force; this is why it is often linked with achievement and success – the desire for which provides a full and intense life experience. Red can speed up the pulse and respiratory rate. All of these are positive aspects of our lives, as long as they are controlled. When the colour red is channelled into spiritual love, it is the strongest of all. The brilliance of bright red captures attention, as is exemplified by red traffic lights, fire engines and shiny red sports cars. In colour therapy, it is a good choice to help overcome melancholia and depression, increase both hormonal and sexual activity and help heal wounds. Red even increases the growth of plants.

Different colours correspond to different frequencies on the electromagnetic spectrum. Pink is the softest vibration of the colour red, which allows the heart centre to feel love without the powerful burning of the red vibration. It is for this reason that salmon pink often represents the colour of universal love. Depending on the shade of pink, this colour can encourage joy and comfort as well as companionship. It is said that people are naturally drawn warmly to those who wear pink.

THE LOVE IMAGE CARD

The image card for the theme of love depicts a single rose, symbol of love, on one side, and is coloured red on the other. The rose can be used as a mandala for meditation – it has been likened to a mandala because of its many petals: when the flower is in full bloom, it resembles a labyrinth pattern. For this purpose you may want to recite the following Love Meditation paragraph, slowly, and record it onto a tape – emphasizing each sentence, and allowing a four- or five-second gap between each sentence.

The tape can be played as you gaze at the image card, to help focus your attention. Hold this image for as long as it is comfortable. When appropriate, slowly open your eyes, and bring yourself back into normal consciousness.

The colour red on the reverse side of the love image card can also be used as a focus of your meditation.

A LOVE MEDITATION: ENTERING THE ROSE

What beauty is this soft red rose, thick and full of petals. Deep inside the petals can be seen a perfect bud, just beginning to open. Look very closely, and a tiny diamond glistening in the centre of the bud can be seen. Slowly close your eyes as you become a point of soft light which gently flows towards the petals. Your light falls on an outer petal, and you become aware of how soft and delicate it feels. The sensation surrounds your light and you feel intoxicated by all this beauty. Now float towards the next inner layer of petals and gently touch it. Notice what you experience. Move deeper into the next layer of colour and scent, and begin to sense the radiance of the light inside the half-closed inner bud. Smell the delicate fragrance. Feel yourself become dancing light as you flow in circular waves about this exquisite flower. Slowly, you are being drawn into the centre of this beauty, and for a while, you become one with the pure crystal diamond light.

THE LOVE MANTRA: 'AH'
ON THE AUDIOTAPE

The chakra associated with the love theme is the heart chakra, or anahata. Many sensitive people have unconsciously covered and hidden it, in order not to be overwhelmed by the realities of everyday life.

While this defensive act serves as a protective coating to avoid being hurt, unfortunately it also blocks the innate ability to give and receive the love that could fill their lives.

The heart chakra is particularly sensitive to the mantra 'Ah'.

By concentrating on your heart chakra, which is located in the same place as the physical heart *(see page 33)*, and continually repeating the sound 'Ah', you will experience a heightened sense of vitality, and what the mystics call 'an opening of the heart'.

This means that you become more open to the quality of love. 'The resonance of "Ah" will become more and more vibrant until your whole being becomes vibrant,' says the Sufi leader Pir Vilyat Inayat Khan. He goes on to say that, if this sound is practised every day, your whole being will become highly vibrant with life and enhanced energy, because the 'Ah' has the powerful effect of expanding consciousness to cosmic dimensions.

MANTRA

आ

'AH'

THE SOUND OF LOVE: 'BUZZING BEES'
ON THE AUDIOTAPE

The sound of buzzing bees was selected as the sound symbol for the theme of Love. Like every other symbol, this one acts on a number of important levels.

In ancient Greece, the beehive was associated with immortality, and often lent its shape to tombs. (At legendary Mycenae, in Greece, lies the so-called Tomb of Agamemnon. Its beehive-like vault rises up thirty feet or more. The acoustics are very odd here; in particular, from a point near the base of the walls, a distinct 'buzzing-bee' type of sound is heard.)

Bees also carry the symbolism of the soul and are, of course, linked with honey – the offering to supreme deities and often associated with love. Bees were believed to impart 'the sweet pain' – Cupid, the god of love, was stung by a bee. Similarly, bees were said to follow Kama, the Hindu god of love.

At another, more literal level, bees are associated with a rose garden; and while listening to their gentle buzzing, you can easily picture yourself strolling in a sunny summer garden full of the scent of roses, and even conjure up the image of a gentle zephyr whispering through the rose-laden garden of love.

Who do you meet there?

~ PEACE ~

Peace is to be found only within, and unless one finds it there one will never find it at all.

RALPH WALDO TRINE

You are lying on the grass on a warm summer day, looking up at the blue sky, alone, with only the beautiful sound of birdsong running through your mind. There is no distraction, nothing but the peace, the warmth and the beauty, and the endless blue sky. If only this could be wrapped up and taken home! In a way it can – by visualizing this scene in meditation, it can be revisited as often as you like.

In fact, any experience which has brought you joy and fulfilment can be recaptured through meditation. In everyday life, peace is usually another story. Sadly, modern life is often filled with obstacles to peace: having to deal with personal and interpersonal relationships, illness, disappointments, tragedies and even betrayals. Bills must be paid, groceries must be bought, along with all the other necessities for survival. Whether in the work environment or at home, much of the time is spent in trying to please others and to live up to their expectations. In addition, we live in the most materialistic society in the world and all the pressures it brings! Where is the peace in all of this?

WHAT IS PEACE?

A rationalist will say that those who think there can be peace live in a fairy tale, and that every day must be lived for what it is, not what they want it to be. Yet most people have a need for peace at a deep, almost unconscious level: and an opportunity to be immersed in peace is essential to the health of the soul.

When real life hits us, very few of us are prepared. How can we deal with the death of a child? How can we explain an action that takes away our material security? What do we do when our husband or wife leaves us for another person? Where is the peace then?

DIVINE PEACE

In reality, we seek a deep level of peace that can absorb all these kinds of tragic or trying circumstances – it has to be the profound peace that 'passeth understanding'. We cannot find the peace we require by attempting to rationalize the vagaries life presents us with. It has to be a transcendental or divine level of peace. In meditation, one can reach a high level of consciousness (the samadhi state) in which one enters this realm of peace or grace. When this condition of consciousness is achieved, all dualities, all unfairness, pain and opposition find their resolution. As impossible as this pinnacle of meditational achievement may seem in our normal state of mind, be assured that it exists as surely as the vast blue sky stretches out beyond even the darkest and angriest of clouds.

So, ultimately, we have to come to terms with change in order to survive change, and be able to grow through the experience. To acquire this ability and understanding, we need to get in touch with our spiritual centre: peace comes from inside. We need an ego to navigate in daily life, but it must not bar access to the spirit, and meditation can help the process.

The reality is that there is no peace outside ourselves. Peace comes from within us, from knowing, trusting and accepting ourselves. Meditation can reveal states of peace that are so all-encompassing that they remain with us, and become part of our lives. In deep meditation, when all mental disturbance is subdued and thought held in abeyance, and when there is no sense of self left (do not be afraid, you do come back!), one can be blessed with a profound transpersonal experience in which one feels a weightless sensation, and one takes off into pure light. Total peace.

Unfortunately, unless we are very advanced spiritual beings, we cannot remain for long in that blissful state of consciousness. And after such transcendental experiences, on re-entering the gross levels of heavy physical reality once more, life can sometimes appear as something of a cosmic joke. Nonetheless, the very opening of that channel in our brain can eventually change our lives to an enormous extent.

One of the negative effects of becoming more aware of ourselves is, sometimes, a strong feeling of guilt concerning particular past actions. After meditating for a while, however, it usually becomes clear that these actions could not have been different. They were necessary for growth: making wrong judgements is indeed a part of the learning experience. Once our awareness surfaces through meditation practice, we can no longer react and behave in the old pattern. After we have forgiven ourselves, we can then take a great stride towards personal peace.

If we really work at it, peace becomes part of our reality. For beginners, this may sound very abstract – a fairy tale. Yet it is a realm of experience that can be accessed through meditation. It is impossible to maintain such a preternatural state of peace in everyday life, however – even for those who have experienced it often. (That would be living in a state of grace and make more saints than heaven could hold!) But once experienced, the powerful memory – the certainty – remains; belief and hope are replaced by knowledge. It can be a lifesaving beacon in times of adversity.

How often, in times of stress and disappointment, are we then able to close our eyes and remember the vast, divine reality of peace dwelling within the singing of the birds and the endless blue sky.

Wordsworth, the nineteenth-century English poet, expressed this with genius in 'Lines Composed a Few Miles Above Tintern Abbey':

... a sense sublime
Of something far more deeply interfused,
Whose dwelling is the light of setting suns,
And the round ocean and the living air,
And the blue sky, and in the mind of man ...

THE SYMBOL OF PEACE: A SKYSCAPE

An expansive skyscape was chosen as an image of peace, rather than some hackneyed, secular 'peace symbol'.

The blue sky is given as a representation of the esoteric heavens. We look up and see the sky as a protective and endless unknown. The enormous space seems to trigger our imagination – helped by the fantastic formations of clouds. We can imagine our spirits drifting with the clouds to far celestial spaces. Ethereal, floating free.

A big sky stretching over a flat landscape is also a profoundly stabilizing, horizontal image, in its own right. It speaks of calmness, tranquillity and expansiveness.

The sky is the ultimate symbol of transcendence and infinity; it is the image of heavenly peace. As we have noted, it is also the transcendental promise that exists beyond the troubled, cloudy skies of everyday life. Many of us will have experienced that exhilarating feeling of taking off in an aircraft from an airport shrouded in dreary, drizzly weather, and buffering through the fog-like atmosphere of the clouds, suddenly to break through into the clear, sunlit canopy of the sky on the far side of the clouds. We can visualize meditation as being like that aircraft, a vehicle that carries us through and beyond the hovering cloudy consciousness of our mundane lives.

THE COLOUR OF PEACE: BLUE

Blue is widely considered to have a psychologically 'cooling' quality, which has been used to calm, subdue and soothe mental stress, and even many physical conditions arising out of that.

In 1930, Dr Oscar Brunler, in Vienna, claimed that the electromagnetic vibration corresponding to a particular shade of blue was the same as the vibrations he picked up from healthy nerve tissue. You can discover for yourself that the contemplation of the colour blue will have a pacifying effect.

The Sanskrit word *nila* is used to describe a special blue color which, according to Dr Max Lüscher, who did extensive work on the psychological implications of colour and devised the Lüscher Colour Test in 1969, creates the most suitable environment for the purposes of meditation. Lüscher's colour analysis showed that blue is chosen as the favourite colour when there is an emotional need for tranquillity and peace.

Blue is the colour most often associated with meditation and spiritual expansion. It has also been associated with truth, devotion and security, as well as being the colour of intuition and the higher mental faculties. Blue rays are said to increase metabolism, build vitality and reduce nervous excitement. If the colour blue is used excessively, however, it may produce a sense of sadness. Indeed, using anything in excess often produces the opposite of what is desired.

In his seminal work, *Theory of Colours,* Goethe describes blue as being a contradiction between excitement and repose. Blue is the colour of the sky, but also of the mountains which we see in the distance, and which have the capacity of drawing our consciousness into infinity. The clear blue sky is both radiant and empty, making it unconditional and without reference or direction, allowing direction and location to manifest within our own consciousness as we gaze at it.

THE PEACE IMAGE CARD

The image card for the theme of peace shows billowing white clouds against a background of blue sky on one side and is coloured blue on the other. Focus on the skyscape scene in order to calm the mind while inducing the sensation of floating in space with the clouds.

For this purpose you may want to recite the following Peace Meditation paragraph slowly and record it onto a tape – emphasizing each sentence, and allowing a four- or five-second gap between sentences. The tape can then be played as you gaze at the image card to help you focus your attention.

Hold this image for as long as it feels comfortable. When it feels appropriate, slowly open your eyes, and bring yourself back into normal consciousness. The colour blue on the reverse side of the peace image card can also be used as a focus point of meditation.

A PEACE MEDITATION: SOARING WITH THE SKYLARK

A skylark's song hovering high and free on a warm, calm summer's afternoon in the rich peace of remote countryside. Let your spirit rise out of your body and join with the joyous song of the skylark. Accompany the pure, wavering notes of birdsong as they rise upwards higher and higher into the vast blue realms of the sky. Upwards through the scatter of quietly floating white, fluffy clouds into the deep blue of endless, silent space beyond. Let that profound blue vastness embrace your entire being. Let the colour enter your body, mind and very soul. Let it exist within you and you within it. Absorb the profound peace of the heavens — the peace and the blueness are one and the same. Enter the profound peace of the heavens; let your mind and soul dwell awhile there, becoming healed and restored. Float gentle and free through the wide blue yonder, through celestial peace and quietude.

THE PEACE MANTRA: 'OM SHANTI' ON THE AUDIOTAPE

The mantra 'Om Shanti' is used by most of the Eastern philosophies to represent the concept and feeling of peace. It is given as a blessing by many of their teachers. This mantra holds within it many of the vibratory sounds used in the single-sound mantras. 'Om' is associated with the creative point (the universal god) and represents the fundamental thought form of all-pervading reality. The same essential idea is contained in the Christian concept of 'the word made flesh'. 'Shanti' means peace, and so together 'Om Shanti' means universal peace on every level.

The repetition of 'Om Shanti' will generate a state of gentle tranquillity and peacer. You can be confident that the collected wisdom of untold generations of meditational practice have ensured that this mantric sound will act as a powerful vibrational vehicle to carry your mind (or your spirit) into the vast levels of cosmic peace. Like any vehicle, it takes a while to learn to drive it. As with all the mantras described, it helps if one continues the silent mental repetition of the mantra at any convenient time during normal waking consciousness — walking, during chores or waiting for a bus! Such regular repetition will eventually produce a resonance that can affect your everyday mental state.

MANTRA

ॐ शांति

'OM SHANTI'

THE SOUND OF PEACE: 'BIRDSONG' ON THE AUDIOTAPE

Birdsong was selected as the background sound for the theme of peace. Imagining oneself in some glorious meadow, serenaded by a chorus of birds, must surely be one of the most peaceful images there are. A skylark hovers high in the sky: its song producing soul-lifting peace.

Research in the late 1980s by Cambridge musician David Hindley has shown that the songs of birds are highly compressed sequences of notes. Hindley had to slow down his tape recordings of a skylark's song by a factor of sixteen in order to make a musical notation of it. He found that a 48-second burst of skylark song ran to almost 13 minutes' worth of sheet music!

In a single day, a few birds can compose the equivalent of hundreds of symphonies composed by human beings.

From his tape recording, Hindley found that the structural principles governing the skylark's song were the same as those underlying the music of Beethoven. Other birds evoke the structural qualities of other composers: the instinctive singing of birds and the creative impulses of the human mind seem to adhere to deep, natural patterns.

As you meditate on the theme of peace, let the profound patterns of birdsong help your soul to take flight.

~ BALANCE ~

*Triumph of higher nature over material desires. The ability
to bring both sides of one's nature into harmony.*

EDEN GRAY

Most of us will never willingly alter our set pattern of believing without question that we are what we think we are. Our ego, our personality, and our endless repetitive routines of daily life feel safe; that is what our culture is all about.

We have life insurance, health insurance and car insurance. There is insurance for pets and insurance for holidays, and we would have insurance against change if it were available. Change is the opposite of security. But we are forced into change when life presents unexpected obstacles. We may lose jobs or fortunes, and we sometimes lose against the unpredicatable violence of the elements when their awesome power is unleashed upon us with sometimes disastrous results.

We think of all this as loss, but it is really just life — and life is about change. Life is ongoing change on every possible level.

When faced with these problems in life, the true self has to emerge and deal with reality. Only then do we find our true persona, the stuff we are really made of. Some people are able to face change with excitement and imagination. Change may make us more alert, more aware of the people and places around us, and more appreciative of the preciousness of life. Most of us, however, just react with feelings of anger, insecurity and fear.

WHAT IS BALANCE?

Every second we live and breathe, some change is taking place. Nothing is static on any level. In our bodies, cells are regenerating and dying; our children are developing physically and mentally, friends may be moving further away, or closer, parents are becoming older; even the atoms in our homes are changing.

The philosophers of India have recognized this for thousands of years: they say life is 'maya', meaning all illusion.

What we believe to be solid and secure is really a phantom curtain made of cobwebs. Life is ever-changing!

To acknowledge the fragile thread by which our life hangs could be a terrifying experience, but meditation will help take the fear and anxiety away – truly.

Acceptance of the true reality of life leads to balance. And balance is freedom.

Pir Vilayat Inayat Khan once expressed it this way: 'All of us are usually swimming upstream against the current. In meditation one learns to flip over and lie back and enjoy floating with the current.'

After meditating for a while, we reach a plateau where we start to see the truth in all that is. Life is as it should be, not what we want it to be. It is time to float instead of swimming for our lives.

Meditation, and the awareness it awakens within us, gives us an opportunity to become a better human being. We are no longer living in a trance state: we start to really see, to hear and to feel.

To really feel, we have to be true to our very essence. We have to drop all the protective masks our ego uses, and simply be. We need to float with the current, knowing that life is just what it is.

We may soon start wanting to help others as well as ourselves. We can finally see beauty in our world and cherish it. We can experience change as exciting – a vibrant opportunity to grow and expand our mind, our heart and even our soul.

Balance is achieved when change is accepted and we go with the flow rather than try to oppose it, as we so often do.

This could be made easier if we were able to accept that *now* is the only reality. We have to try to understand that if we are really in it, really in the now, nothing is insurmountable. When we reach the point of being able to accept change, we will no longer have to worry about past events or future possibilities

The Tibetan teacher, Ngakpa Ch. Wgyam, tells us: 'Since nothing is permanent or secure, pride and arrogance are encumbrances we can do without. The only stable ground we can find is by establishing Insecurity as our Security.'

THE DYNAMICS OF BALANCE

Balance is not a static, passive state. The tightrope walker is constantly adjusting his weight and posture in order to find the central, balanced axis of his body.

In meditational terms, this is well represented in that old form of dynamic, ecstatic practice performed by 'whirling dervishes'. This Sufi sect adopts time-honoured postures that allow them to whirl rapidly without losing their balance, sending their minds into profound altered states.

The whirling dervish holds his right hand aloft, palm up, as if receiving divine energy which is transmuted by his body and then directed by his lowered left hand, palm down, towards the earth. He visualizes a central axis running through his body that enables him to maintain balance as he spins.

It is claimed that the tilt of the dervish's head represents the angle of the Earth's axis, in which case the turning body is analagous to the rotation of the planet itself.

Such Sufi adepts can spin for long periods of time without getting dizzy, and this, despite the fact that the eyes are kept open while the whirling takes place. The ecstasy can only be achieved if the balance is maintained.

We mention this form of profound meditation based on balance simply as an illustration.

The method itself requires prolonged practice and expert teaching; if some readers wish to engage in it, we advise them to seek proper, spiritual training.

THE SYMBOL OF BALANCE: THE WATERFALL

The waterfall was chosen as the image for the balance theme, because it so wonderfully expresses the dynamics of balance.

The ancient Chinese would use narrow gullies of water to verify that their astronomical observatories were perfectly level. Water always seeks its own level, and comes to rest only in a state of balance.

The waterfall, therefore, is a powerfully dynamic image of the quest for balance — balance in action, if you like. The surging waters leading to the great fall can represent our minds, churning and spinning with indecision before the fear and chaos of the daily turmoil. The powerful descent

of the water can represent the release of the power of consciousness as mind finds its own, natural level — which can only be the point of supreme balance — provided we do not interrupt the dynamics. It is a tricky juggling act!

THE COLOUR OF BALANCE: GREEN

The primary colours yellow and blue are polar opposites, and at their centre, out of the equal mix of both of them — or balance point — the colour green is produced. Green is pleasing to the eyes. It represents harmony and balance. Green is a cooling, soothing and calming colour, both physically and mentally.

According to colour psychologists, green is a passive and self-regulating colour, which has an astringent effect physiologically. It has the universal appeal of nature — in the sense of its balance and normality. Green is the colour most associated with life. Each spring, nature cloaks herself in a dazzling display of many wonderful shades of green. Our emotions come into balance when we immerse ourselves in the rich greenery of the countryside — the fields, the hills, the trees.

In colour therapy, green is said to reduce nervous and muscular tension. It is good for concentration and contemplation. Green is considered to be the universal colour for healing, able to restore a sense of wellbeing and balance.

THE BALANCE IMAGE CARD

The image card for the theme of Balance shows a waterfall cascading over a rocky ledge, merging into the pool of water beneath, where it finds its own level or balance. The back of the card is coloured green.

The waterfall image can be used as a focus for a meditation. For this purpose, you may want to recite the Balance Meditation below, slowly, and record it on to a tape – emphasizing each sentence, and allowing a four- or five-second gap between sentences. The tape can then be played as you gaze at the image cards, to help you focus your attention.

You can hold this image for as long as it feels comfortable. When you feel it is appropriate, slowly open your eyes and bring yourself back into normal consciousness.

The colour green covers the reverse side of the waterfall image card, and can also be used as a focus point of meditation.

THE BALANCE MANTRA 'E' ON THE AUDIOTAPE

The high 'E' sound is used to open the third eye or, in meditational terms, to give us the ability to 'see' more clearly. The third eye is associated with vision.

Seeing more clearly on a mundane level can certainly help us to be more balanced in our individual lives, as well as in the way we function in society.

Esoterically, the brow chakra, or third eye, when activated through meditation, acquires the gift of telepathy and can beam light out with tremendous penetrating power.

This, of course, is a mental image perceived internally. The activating effect of the vibrations of the high 'E' sound opens up the meditator to the possibility of psychic vision.

The high 'E' sound comes from the mantra 'Ya Alim' – the 'i' in 'Alim' is pronounced as if saying the letter 'e' in the alphabet. This sound represents supreme understanding, or, in the memorable words of Pir Vilayat Inayat Khan, it stands for: 'the understanding behind the understanding, the eyes behind our eyes.'

This goes beyond perception or cognition, into the realm of illumination.

BALANCE MEDITATION: FINDING YOUR LEVEL

Water, yielding and fluid, yet stronger than stone, finds its way always to its lowest level. Water is forever on a journey to the level of balance, of equilibrium. Feel yourself flow with the water, fall with the water, roar with the water on your fluid, sinuous journey through and over the obstacles of life to the flat, level surface of primordial balance, the inner lake where all things have their essential level. Let yourself pour down to your inner level of balance, and flow into that deep inner lake. Feel the turbulence you have travelled through subside. Dissolve into the placid vastness of the lake, spreading out into a state of perfect balance, perfect calm. You can no longer fall. You have found your natural level.

THE SOUND OF BALANCE: 'ROARING WATER' ON THE AUDIOTAPE

The sound of roaring water was selected as the acoustic ambience for the theme of balance, not only because it obviously relates to the visual symbol, but also because the nature of the sound can actually help your brain rhythms to become more organized – and in this way lead to a balanced mental condition.

A large waterfall, or a rushing mountain stream, provides the sort of sound known as 'pink noise' – similar to white noise, but with rhythmic elements that help to 'drive' certain brain rhythm frequencies.

When you listen to one, the sound will first resemble radio static, for it is technically a similar sound. Soon, though, it will become more organized or 'tuned', and from it may come sounds like voices, or deep, rhythmic pulses.

Analysis was recently conducted on the sound of waterfalls by British electronics expert Rodney Hale, as part of investigations into the effect of the environment on human consciousness carried out by writer and researcher Paul Devereux. The research revealed a regular pattern of acoustic frequencies at a level of about 5 Hz (five cycles per second), reaching up to 7 Hz: which corresponds to the alpha brain rhythm frequency range *(see page 95)*.

Such sounds can actually entrain, or 'drive', brain rhythms, and so are very helpful in producing certain mental states. In this case, alpha brain rhythms are the ones we want to cultivate, because biofeedback investigations have shown that they precede the meditative state. Alpha rhythms are the brain's doorway to meditation.

One of the most beautiful associations made with the sound of rushing water is found in the German novelist Hermann Hesse's deeply spiritual book, *Siddhartha*. At the climax, the hero Siddhartha, after a lifetime of seeking spiritual truth and believing that his quest is hopeless, stays with an old ferryman sage called Vasudeva.

One day, while the two men are crossing the river, Vasudeva tells Siddhartha to listen to the rushing water. Siddhartha hears the 'many-voiced song' of the river: it laughs and cries and seems full of thousands of voices. Suddenly, Siddhartha reaches a moment of balance, and all the voices merge into one great sound – the river is singing the great song of life. Siddhartha's sense of self similarly dissolves into the flow, his desperate clinging to sensual objects of desire ceases, and he gains the unity of vision that opens the door to enlightenment.

When you meditate on the theme of balance, the sound of rushing water will remind you to allow yourself to float with the current of your life.

MANTRA

'E'

~ TRANSFORMATION ~

The greatest benefactors we have we regard
as our greatest adversaries

H.E.BUTLER

Whether we like it or not, life is a constant process of transformation – sometimes sudden and dramatic, yet at other times so slow and subtle that we barely notice it taking place. We all know the experience of meeting up with old friends after a long time without seeing them. The effect the years have had on them are immediately obvious to us – sometimes causing quite a shock. On the other hand, when we look in the mirror each day we do not notice the effects of our own ageing.

Changes in our circumstances can come about through deliberate effort on our part, or by the effects of other people's actions, or alterations in conditions. And transformation can occur within us too: we may change our opinion about something, or see someone in a new light. We may shift from being depressed to being more hopeful, or vice versa. However change comes, whether it is swift and sudden or gradual and progressive, whether affecting us inwardly our outwardly, change is merely the natural and fundamental basis of life.

WHAT IS TRANSFORMATION?

Every part of our body is undergoing transformation continually. Molecules are taken into the system – in the form of food – and broken down by the system almost as quickly. What is needed is utilized, and what is not needed is eliminated. There is a constant dichotomy between transmutation and cohesion. And then there is death.

The word 'transformation' may seem a peculiar word to describe death. After years of meditating, however, it becomes clear that it is the most appropriate description of the event our culture teaches us to think of as finality. Webster defines 'to transform' as: 'to change the form of – to change an outward shape or semblance … Physics: to change one form of energy into another. To become transformed.'

Hindus believed that death was not a release, but merely an interval between periods of conscious existence. We live, we die; our bodies are machines and our parts wear out; or so we are taught. Our egos may believe this, but our spirit knows the reality. And truly, why would we want to exist forever? Is not one lifetime of experience enough for one ego?

Other religions and philosophies accept this reality and understand that death is the natural progression of our lives. Our Western understanding of death has always been associated with pain, loss, sorrow and endings. Think of how most of us react to the promise of death. Yet many cultures see death in a totally different light. They greet it with acceptance and understanding and, yes, even anticipation. Our culture sees the ending only in negative ways: how many of us really believe we are going to heaven?

We rarely associate death with positive and beautiful concepts. In meditation, we should be sure to do so. Just as we shift out of everyday consciousness in deep meditation, and find ourselves in a very different time and space, so too is death a shift of consciousness. Believe this as you meditate, and you may come to know it as a truth. A different picture of death evolves; you begin to sense that there is much more. If death is a shift in consciousness, and we can experience these states while in physical form, death loses its terror.

The Egyptians referred to this knowledge of death-in-life as 'coming forth triumphantly by day', a more fitting title to the text commonly known as *The Egyptian Book of the Dead*. Rather than being written by one person, it is a compilation of funerary texts written and added to by many different priests during the time of the pharaohs, spanning a period of approximately 4,000 years. As ruler of the dead, Osiris was also recognized as the principle of regeneration – his symbol was the abundant growing corn, a symbol of transformation.

The Egyptians also possessed the greatest symbolical language there has ever been for transformation – alchemy. The word derives from the Arabic *Al Kimiya*, meaning the magical craft of the Black Country, a reference to the dark soil of the Nile delta.

The aims of alchemy were to transmute base metals to gold, to discover the nature of the philosopher's stone with which further transmutation could be effected, and to find the elixir of life. These aims could be taken at the literal, exoteric level – the attempt to produce gold from metal and to find or produce objective substances for the elixir. But, by correspondence, these features and processes were also applied to inner, psychological or spiritual changes within the alchemist.

The true alchemical processs was essentially sacramental – an outward side of inward grace. It was an obscure and trying business, and the alchemical texts abound with complex symbolism and brain-teasing commentaries. Most appear as gibberish – a term, appropriately, derived from one of the early Arabian alchemists, Geber.

The essence of the alchemical work was the union of sulphur and mercury which was imaged as a marriage. The sulphur and mercury themselves were symbols of masculine and feminine, the king and queen, sun and moon, gold and silver. The outcome or 'child' of this union was the philosopher's stone, which itself holds the key to transmutation. Hence the alchemical marriage can be seen as the supreme metaphor in the Western philosophy of transformation.

During meditation, we are trying to transmute the lead of mundane consciousness into the gold of higher awareness. In this context, death is seen as the ultimate process of transformation – from gross matter to the etheric realms of spirit.

In a spiritual sense, the raw material that the alchemist worked with was himself. Carl Jung recognized the world of alchemy as a psychological and spiritual quest towards unity of self.

How did we come to fear this transition? Leaving our bodies might well be an enormous relief. It could be like a beautiful butterfly-soul breaking out of its cocoon – the soul is free.

Look at all the ancient symbols showing us the concept of death and rebirth. The sun, rising every morning after its death at sunset, has been celebrated from neolithic times. The phœnix rises from its ashes. And so on.

Humanity has always sensed the concept of a death-rebirth cycle: death as transformation. Our culture alone inculcates the idea of the final end of consciousness at the final end of physical life. Yet energy cannot be destroyed – it can only transform. And is not consciousness energy?

THE SYMBOL OF TRANSFORMATION: LIGHTNING

The image of lightning selected for this theme expresses the idea of transformation on a number of different levels. In an electrical storm, the invisible drift of electricity between the clouds and the surface of the earth can be transformed into vivid visibility by a bolt of lightning.

What was slow and diffuse suddenly becomes focused and instantaneous. This can happen with our mental processes, too: we say we have a 'flash of inspiration', or a 'flash of recognition'. In a flash, we can become transformed.

When lightning strikes the earth, it charges the ground with regenerative power – the force of transformation.

The electrical storms of spring help revitalize the dormant land from which emerge beauty and life. We see the growth of flowers and trees and the green mantle of grass that covers much of the land on our planet. The animal kingdom is busy having its young, and a new cycle of life is starting once again.

These images reflect the power and secrets of transformation.

The power of the lightning bolt symbolizes the regenerative and unknowable secrets displayed by this enormous energy.

THE COLOUR OF TRANSFORMATION: PURPLE

Purple is at the high end of the colour vibration spectrum. It is a secondary colour, formed by mixing red and blue – a combination of the most active and the most tranquil of the colours. Esoterically, it represents a culmination of life's lessons: how we have been able to grow and, hopefully, how we overcome the trials of daily life.

According to the Lüscher Colour Test, a preference for purple indicates that you enjoy the finer things in life, but are also tactful and warm by nature, with a high regard for integrity. Your emotions are kept in control, and honesty is of the utmost importance.

Purple represents wisdom and understanding, and has always been the chosen colour of royalty and religion. Royal people are said to have been 'born to the purple'. These social associations are reflections of the colour's symbolic link with spiritual awareness. In the rituals of some of our religions, dark purple has always been in evidence when transformation – death – is being celebrated, reminding us that death is part of the natural process of life.

THE TRANSFORMATION IMAGE CARD

The image card for the theme of Transformation shows bolts of lightning striking the mountainous ground below. The lightning bolt is used here to represent sudden and often permanent change, and makes an ideal focal point for meditation on the theme of Transformation. For this purpose, you may want to recite the following Transformation Meditation paragraph, slowly, and record it on to a tape – emphasizing each sentence, and allowing a four- or five-second gap between sentences. The tape can then be played back as you gaze at the image cards, to help you focus your attention. You can hold this image for as long as it feels comfortable. When appropriate, slowly open your eyes and bring yourself back into a state of normal consciousness.

TRANSFORMATION MEDITATION: BECOMING THE LIGHTNING

The heavy atmosphere before a storm, like the density of the material world forming the physical cocoon of the soul, of the mind. Suddenly the heavy tension is punctuated and relieved by a great flash of lightning followed by the rumble of its thunder. The thunder tells of the great transformation of energies that have just occurred. Become the lightning! Roll with the thunder! Ride the great waves of transformational energies and break out of that dense cocoon to become the butterfly of the spirit, like the butterflies of summer that follow the reviving spring storms. Feel the power of transformational forces flow through you, body and soul. Feel how transformation is simply the act of redirecting, redistributing your energies. Let your mind flash through the dark skies of the material world. Move from darkness to light. Like the lightning bolt, harness the forces of change within yourself.

The colour purple on the reverse side of the transformation image card can also be used as a focus point of meditation.

THE TRANSFORMATION MANTRA 'AUM' ON THE AUDIOTAPE

Contained within the mantra 'Aum' are the three most important vibratory sounds, which represent three periods of time, three states of consciousness or entire existence (A = awaking state, U = dream state, M = sleeping state) to help us reach the highest state of consciousness.

We can liken this to the metaphor of three separate notes being played on a violin (or perhaps more appropriately, the Indian stringed instrument known as the sitar which is thought to be able to directly affect the 'energy body' of the human being). Each note although struck separately, combines to form a vibrational whole which we recognize as a musical sound. So, rather than concentrating on one centre, as with the mantras associated with the previous themes, 'Aum' vibrates throughout the physical body and what esotericists call our etheric body – a supposed energy field which resides outside the physical body, and appears as a halo in representations of angels and saints.

There are three separate sounds within 'Aum' which combine to express the principle of totality.

MANTRA

ओ ३म्

'AUM'

'Aum' acts as a metaphysical dynamo to move us from a state of incompletion to one of greater unity. So, when our being is filled with the vibration of the 'Aum', the energy impels us towards a transformational experience. It has the rare ability to force us out of our gross physicality into the transcendental state of bliss.

THE SOUND OF TRANSFORMATION 'THUNDER AND RAIN' ON THE AUDIOTAPE

The keynote sound chosen to support the theme of transformation is thunder. Thunder accompanies lightning with its transformational power. It is the sound of vast forces in nature transforming themselves from one kind of energy to another.

Thunder and its frequent acoustical accompaniment, the roar of rain, also provides another example of pink noise, the kind of external sound that occurs naturally in nature which can help entrain alpha beta rhythms, so important for the development of meditative states

Thunder is also the sound of one of the greatest cycles in nature – the water cycle, in which rain falls from the heavens and makes things grow. It fills the rivers and streams which in turn rush to the ocean, where the heat of the sun draws water into the clouds once again. This is the great cycle of life – the ultimate miracle of transformation.

HOW TO USE THE MEDITATIONAL TOOLS

THE IMAGE CARDS

Each card is illustrated on one side with an image that is pertinent to the particular theme it represents; on the other side is a corresponding colour. The most direct way of using an image card is to stand it vertically in front of you, at a comfortable distance for your vision, with either the image or the colour side facing you.

The cards can be used for meditation in several different ways. The most effective and simple ones are given below.

Using the image

To start your theme meditation, assume a meditational posture. Then make sure that you practise one of the breathing techniques described earlier, to achieve total relaxation.

When you are ready, look in a relaxed but unwavering manner into, rather than at, the image. The idea is to imprint it in your short-term memory. After a while, close your eyes and try to visualize the image in your mind's eye, thinking of the theme it is related to at the same time.

Place yourself in the picture. You may be looking at the scene as a third party, or you may find yourself actually inside it.

Turn it into a kind of virtual reality environment inside your head. Allow the scene to unfold, and be receptive to any messages that come forth. The themes are so rich that you will most likely find them inexhaustible.

Using colour

Another way of working with the cards is to use the reverse, coloured side. Remember that each theme has a colour correspondence. Set up your chosen card with the colour side facing you. Then visualize and focus upon it, in much the same way as you did using the image side of the card.

The colour cards may be used to meditate in association with the particular theme they represent. But you may choose to meditate upon a colour simply because it has special significance for you. Or again, you may prefer simply to focus on a selected colour in the abstract, as it were, to see where it might lead you.

In dreams

Another particularly powerful way of using the cards is to look at the selected picture before closing your eyes and going to sleep. This exercise needs to be repeated over quite a long period of time. In this way you will internalize the imagery, and may even begin to dream about it. Using the cards in this way should make your meditation sessions even more effective.

THE AUDIOTAPE

Each of the themes in this kit has a mantra and ambient sound related to it, which are reproduced on the audiotape. The ambient sounds are found on the tape directly following the entonement of the mantras.

Select the theme of your choice and set up the relevant audiotape so that it is ready to play. The theme sounds will be heard in the same order as they appear in this book. There are 14 minutes of playing time for each of the theme sounds.

Settle into meditative posture, either with your eyes closed, or using one of the visual aid methods described above.

To begin with, however, it is best to use each type of aid one at a time. When you have become more proficient, then you can experiment with mixing the modes.

The mantra for a selected theme will be uttered at the beginning of the soundtrack, so that you can listen to it before entoning it for yourself. You can use the mantra as your cue for both beginning and ending the meditation. Let the sound fill your being as you are focusing on the theme.

The evocative, ambient sounds you will hear following the mantra are not designed to describe the theme, but to provide an acoustic trigger for associations that will strengthen your attempts at a visualization. They will help you to place yourself inside the scene.

For each theme, the soundtrack will end with the mantra being intoned once more.

WHERE TO GO FROM HERE

Now that you have learned the basic principles of theme-oriented meditation and how they can operate at different sensory and mental levels, start with the theme that you feel applies more specifically to your preferences and needs, and proceed from there.

With practice, you will find that each of the themes presented in this book is a gateway into a rich garden of the mind. In due course you will want to develop other themes of your own choosing – the actual construction of the aspects of a theme can in itself be a highly instructive exercise.

Before you reach such advanced usage of meditational themes, however, you must first go on to explore other meditative techniques, which you will find in the next chapter.

CHAPTER THREE

SINGLE-POINT AND GUIDED MEDITATION

Constantly in meditation, by whatever form,
technique or method, we find we are opening ourselves
towards the Light.

SIR GEORGE TREVELYAN

This chapter provides a range of simple meditation techniques which include single-point focus, the use of visualization and guided imagery among other methods.

No one technique is better than another. It is for the beginner to find those best suited to her or him. What is important is to feel comfortable with the meditational method you choose. Trial and error is the only way to come to a decision.

Before you start practising any meditation technique, however, always remember that it is essential to relax the body.

Use one of the breathing techniques discussed earlier; or simply take several slow, deep breaths, and send them throughout your whole body, focusing on relaxing it all at once.

SINGLE-POINT MEDITATION

Single-point meditation demands strict concentration on a single object or idea – in contrast to more intricate guided meditations, enabling the mind to eliminate all the chatter that is usually taking place.

Unless the mind is fully tuned in, it is like a radio receiver picking up a lot of unnecessary static. Focusing the mind by means of single-point meditation is like carefully tuning the radio until it is receiving only one station: it is finding the correct signal among all the noise. The steady glow of a candle flame is the ideal object to use for this method. A candle is provided in the kit.

HOW TO USE THE CANDLE

Place the candle in an appropriate candle-holder on a small table or surface in front of where you are sitting. Ideally, nothing should be visible in the background that could divert your attention. A dark backdrop is best. Also, be sure that the candle is not placed too near an open window or air source, such as a fan or heater, so that there is no danger of the flame going out during meditation.

Light the candle, and assume a comfortable sitting position. Allow yourself to relax as you gaze at the candle. Do this for several minutes. Keep your attention on the brilliant, steady flame long enough to ensure that you can reproduce its image in your mind's eye. Then close your eyes and 'see' the candle flame.

Concentrate strongly upon the image, trying to see every detail and aspect of it. Notice the varying colours in the flame, the corona which surrounds it, its occasional flicker. You will soon become single-pointed in your concentration.

When you are in a focused, calm, relaxed but attentive state, you can gently introduce a word, an idea, an image or a theme (your own or one of those suggested in this kit) upon which to meditate. Try and identify the mental focus of your meditation with the candle flame – which you should still be gazing at.

If your attention wavers, return gently to the image of the flame. If you cannot manage it, open your eyes and focus on the real flame once more, and repeat the exercise.

Use the glowing point of light as a leash to recall your wayward mind: use it to bring your attention back to the focus of the flame. Identify with it. Become its essence .Feel the sensation of light and heat and power that is the flame.

Once you are comfortable with the sensation, you may remain in that state for as long as twenty minutes. After a while, your consciousness will naturally drift back to its normal waking state, bringing with it an enormous sense of peace and tranquillity.

WHAT SINGLE-POINT MEDITATION ACHIEVES

As you become more adept at reaching your single-point objective, you will probably look forward to this vacation from the normal concept of time and space.

The flame of a candle can be used as a representation of all fire images.

If you have ever stared into a burning log fire, or a campfire, even for a short while, you will know how transfixing it can be, as you become more and more drawn into the flames.

Images emerge and shapes occur in the flickering light. The flame can spark the imagination.

Allow the creativity of your imagination to flow. You will soon discover that new ideas, new understanding, and even solutions to old problems can manifest.

Using the candle in this way is one example of what can be achieved by single-point meditation.

Single-pointedness — the ability to focus all thought onto one object — can and will be achieved with time and patience.

As a direct result of practising, you will actually be able to observe your powers of concentration improve — until one day, you yourself will become the object of your meditation.

A WORD OF ADVICE

Do not despair if you occasionally get distracted, particularly when you are starting to learn this technique. There is never any need to feel self-doubt. This happens to even well-seasoned meditators.

With discipline and practice, you will soon be able to stay focused for longer and longer periods. When a distraction occurs, let it pass without dwelling on it. This will enable you to return more easily to the one-pointed state.

GUIDED MEDITATION

Guided meditation techniques consist of using sight, visual imagination, and even feeling, as objects of meditation. Several different techniques can be used for guided imagery or visualization — mental images deliberately formed to guide you on your journey to whatever goal you may have in mind. You can be working on your own or in a group. If you are working in a group, the most experienced member will usually lead the rest, by speaking the visualization. Some groups, however, prefer to use a pre-recorded tape of a journey, so that everyone can experience the meditation.

The focus of the journey is always the individual. It usually starts off with the individual (you) ascending a hill, or a ladder, or crossing a bridge, or following a path. The goal is to lead the meditator toward higher consciousness where insight can be gained, which will ultimately provide a deeper understanding of the self.

While the guided imagery is the same for everyone, the experience will, of course, be unique to each person. Once you have participated a few times in a guided imagery meditation, you may want to develop your own personal visualization, utilizing images that are most meaningful to you. For example, if there is a particular place in nature that you have found inspiring, you can use that as part of your guided imagery. It is always much easier to conjure up the memory of some place where you have already been, than to construct scenes in your mind's eye from scratch.

THE GARDEN

To help you get started, here is the outline of a full-guided visualization as an example. It is based on an imaginary garden, described opposite. You may want to try to visualize it initially as it is written. Later on, you may prefer to create your own. As you read the text and start on your journey, focus on this imaginary garden. Allow all of your senses to become involved in the experience. In addition to visualizing the imagery, listen to the sounds, feel the path beneath your feet, smell the fragances that accompany the scene.

If you like, you can read out and record this, or any other visualizations suggested in this chapter, on to a tape, which you can then use at any time to help lead you into your meditation practice.

When taping a visualization, be sure to speak slowly and clearly, leaving distinct pauses where there are commas. Additional commas have intentionally been placed in the text of the visualizations provided, specifically to allow for this.

Also, allow a few seconds pause at the end of each sentence.

Or you may prefer to have someone else read and record the visualization on to the tape for you: some people find listening to their own voice too distracting.

Just before you start your meditation, remember that it is most important to be in a comfortable position, and to use one of the breathing techniques discussed earlier to relax your body.

VISUALIZATION: THE GARDEN

Take a few deep breaths. You are walking down a beautiful flower-lined, red brick path, which leads towards a small footbridge, visible in the distance. As you walk towards the bridge, take time to inhale the beautiful fragrance of the flowers as you pass. You know as you approach the bridge, that when you cross it you will be stepping into a new dimension of consciousness. This idea excites you. As you step on to the first stone of the foot-bridge, you are immersed in the colour red, for this is a rainbow bridge, on which you will pass through all the colours of the spectrum, drawing their energy into your being. You will be bathed in changes of rich colour with each few strides you take. So, as you move forward, the colour red fills your being with positive energy and power. As you walk further along, you enter the colour orange. Inhale the colour orange, and fill your being with its vibrational energy. This energy represents thoughtfulness and consideration for others. Let this concept dwell in your mind for a moment. Another few steps forward on the bridge take you into the yellow vibration. The colour yellow represents the energy of the sun. As you inhale this vibration you are enhancing your health and well being. As you proceed along the bridge, the pure colour of emerald green embraces you. Inhale slowly and gently, and allow the healing green vibration to enter into your being. The green vibration is helpful, strong and friendly. Continuing along the bridge, you will enter the peaceful blue light of spirit. Wrap this cloak of colour around you and proceed onwards. Soon you will find yourself immersed in the deepening hues of indigo until you are bathed in a rich purple, which will bring you closer to your highest consciousness. As you step off the little footbridge, onto the shore, the energies from all the colours whirl together into brilliant white light that remains with you, illuminating you within and without as you walk onwards. Take a deep breath. As you look around, you will find yourself in a magical garden. It is filled with birdsong, and wondrously-glowing flowers, trees displaying lush, dense foliage and all manner of fruits, and many beautifully carved statues. Take one of the white stone paths that wind through

the garden, and find an inviting little seat tucked into a bower. Sit comfortably there, observing the beauty of nature all around you. Your mind is quiet, still and peaceful. Your heart is full of joy. You are radiating the white light which you have absorbed. After a while, you will see a being walking along the path towards you, and you realize this is a manifestation of your spirit guide or guardian angel. Invite this being to sit with you for a while. You will find that you are able to communicate with this being without the use of words....

At this point, a silence of approximately 10 minutes should follow. If you are recording the visualization, leave a blank space of about the same length of time on the tape.

This period of silence will allow you, within your meditation, to ask your own questions and then to receive the appropriate answers, and for some of the time just to sit quietly with this being who silently radiates such profound love and kindness.

...When your time with the guardian angel or spirit of wisdom seems to be at an end, offer thanks, rise from the seat, and with a feeling of lightness, find your way back to the path that leads back to the bridge, which you can clearly see before you.

As you cross over the bridge, you will again walk through the colours of the rainbow, this time starting with the colour purple. As before, inhale, bringing within yourself the energies of each of these colours. As you step onto the bridge, the white light whirls through and around you, separating out into the rich purple colour ... as you walk on, you are bathed in the peaceful blue ... the healing green ... the energizing yellow ... and the warm, compassionate orange... As you pass through the colour red, and place your foot once again on the brick footpath, you have completed the circle of your guided visualization.

...As you walk back along the footpath, you gradually return to your normal consciousness. When you are ready, open your eyes. You feel invigorated, and at peace with yourself.

Sharing your experiences is an important and fun part of meditation. If you are meditating on your own, you may instead want to keep a journal of your experiences. Try to describe as fully as possible your emotions and thoughts as you walked across the bridge and entered the garden. What was your feeling when you first saw your spirit guide? What did your spirit guide look like?

Did you feel different when you walked back across the bridge? If you have done this meditation more than once (it is advisable to do so – once a week would be suitable), notice if you meet the same spirit guide each time. Keep a record of what happens. Feel free to change any aspects of the visual journey, especially if you are making the tape for your own use rather than for a group. For example, if there are specific flowers that you enjoy, visualize those along the path. Build features into the journey that are specific to you.

CLIMBING THE MOUNTAIN

This is another outline for a guided meditation, although not a full-guided one but on you may want to elaborate on for yourself. It will take you on a visual journey where you ascend the highest mountain your mind can conceive.

VISUALIZATION: CLIMBING THE MOUNTAIN

 Imagine yourself climbing towards the glacial wastes of a Himalayan peak, surrounded by the crystal clarity of the light high above the clouds. As you scale each new level in your climb, you will sense your mind ascending higher, towards increasingly expansive states of consciousness. Allow yourself a few moments at each of the levels to reflect on its particular significance.

When you reach the summit, find a comfortable place to sit. Observe Pir Vilayat Khan's 'cool transcendental light [...] of very high altitudes, almost frozen, immaculate and diaphanous, rising like a fountain,' and enjoy the high altitude of the mind. Here is the place for silent contemplation and a sense of unity. You may decide to invite your spirit guide at this point, or just sit on your own, entering the profound silence you find in this rarefied atmosphere. When you are ready, start your descent, making a brief stop at each level along the way.

It is worth noting that, because of the power of their symbolism, physical mountains were often selected as locations for the practice of meditation by ancient spiritual orders. For example, from the earliest times in Japan there was the tradition of the gyo-ja, the mountain ascetic. In the eighth century Buddhism developed the 'nature wisdom school' which sought enlightenment from being close to nature in the mountains. This resulted in the emergence of the Order of Ascetics.

A word of caution: if you are normally afraid of heights, or do not like climbing, it would be best to use another concept. Some people might like to visualize themselves going up in a lift or elevator, making brief stops at key floors along their way to an exotic tropical roof garden. The ideas are as endless as your own imagination!

PATH-WALKING TO TIPHARETH

This is a guided meditation outline based on the kabbalistic Tree of Life, a powerful tool for all forms of visualization and meditation.

You may want to do some further reading on this rich and complex subject *(see Appendix)*, and develop your own meditation techniques as you learn more about it.

Tiphareth represents beauty. A simple visualization is given here of an inner journey to Tiphareth, one of the sephiroth (holy emanations) of the Tree of Life.

You may want to record this visualization. If you do, remember to pause at each comma, and to stop for a few seconds at the end of each sentence.

VISUALIZATION: PATH-WALKING TO TIPHARETH

You are in a walled garden, standing on a large, green lawn, edged with flowers of many colours. The sun is directly overhead, it is high noon and you throw no shadow. Look at the walls of the garden. They are made of ancient blocks of stone, golden yellow in colour. These walls seem half as old as time itself. They are punctuated at various intervals by great wooden doors, with large black iron rings as handles. All the doors are closed. As you look around, you note that there are three doors on each of three walls, and a single door on the fourth wall which is heavily barred. You walk over to one of the unbarred doors and try turning its great iron ring, but you cannot open the door. You try another door, but you cannot open that either. You realize that you cannot open any of these doors by yourself. Without your being aware of it, a white-haired and white-robed being has walked up to you across the lawn. This being radiates compassion, and smiles at you. You understand that he will be your companion. He leads you towards one of the walls with three doors, and opens the centre one. He signals you to walk through. As

you do so, a fearsome-looking man appears in front of you, dressed in the armour of an ancient soldier, carrying a large sword. He blocks your way. He asks you where you are going. You answer that you wish to walk to Tiphareth…

Remain silent for three or four minutes here.

If the soldier figure in your mind's eye does not disappear from your imagination, this means that it refuses to get out of your way. In which case, visualize returning to the walled garden, and watch your companion close the door. You will thank him. He will smile and walk off out of sight behind you.

As you stroll across the lawn, you slowly return to normal consciousness and open your eyes.

Turn off the tape. This may occur a number of times at first in attempting this visualization.

When, or if, the figure does remove itself from your view, proceed. Visualize walking on beyond the door along a pathway. Then read on, or listen to the tape.

....*The path stretches straight ahead of you. As you walk along, look carefully at the path. It is made of flagstones. They are bright white stones, and do not seem heavily worn. Glance at the rich deep blue sky, then look to your right and to your left as you walk along the path. You can see trees, and flowers all around. Brightly coloured birds can be seen among the tree branches, or flitting between the trees. As you walk along the straight, white-stoned path beneath the rich blue sky, listen to the songs of the birds, the contented hum of bees. Feel the warmth of the sun on your body. Walk on. With each step you feel more joyful. With each step you leave all your normal worries and fears and doubts further and further behind. You continue walking along the white, straight path amongst the flowers and trees, beneath the rich and radiant blue sky, listening to the birdsong and the humming bees. As you walk along, you see something glinting in the distance ahead. You walk closer and closer to it.*

Gradually, you see the path comes to a great paved circle from which seven other white stone paths radiate in all directions, disappearing among the trees and flowers. In the centre of the circle paved with white stone is a huge fountain. You slowly walk around it. It is a fantastic, carved stone structure from the top of which jet out great streamers of water. These jets of water arc up against the rich blue sky, then cascade back, wetting the stone structure, returning underground with a laughter-like sound through the openings around the stone base of the fountain. You look up at this beautiful fountain. The water sparkles in a myriad colours against the deep blue sky. The droplets look like jewels as they shower down towards the base of the fountain. Here you see a rich red ruby... there a glistening green droplet. Everywhere are sparkling white diamond-like drops of water. As you walk around this fountain, your eye catches brief glimpses of soft rainbows in the water mist. You circle the fountain until you are back on the path along which you came. You know it is time to leave this wonderful place, but you know you will come again whenever you can. You walk back along the long straight white path, enjoying the sunlit surroundings, until you see the doorway into the walled garden ahead of you.

You realise that you had forgotten about your white-haired, white-robed companion, who had been silently walking behind you. He now overtakes you and opens the wooden door for you. You enter the walled garden, and watch your companion close the door. You thank him. He smiles at you, then walks out of sight behind you. As you stroll across the lawn, you gradually return to normal consciousness. You open your eyes. You feel happy and fulfilled.

VIRTUAL OBJECT VISUALIZATION

Visualization can also be used for single-point meditation. Rather than staring at a physical object which is placed in front of you – like the flame of a candle – you can visualize any object in your mind's eye.

Concentrate on the visualized 'virtual' object, examining its design, texture and scent (if appropriate) in much the same way as you would if the object was actually placed in front of you.

The object you choose to visualize may be something that you remember from your past, or something that you would like to gain a better understanding of. Again, the possibilities are many. Whatever you decide on, it is important not to bring emotion into the meditation. Focus on the object as you would on something that you have never seen before, from a completely detached place. Concentrate on what impression you receive – images, thought forms or even words – rather than what you can project on it.

HEALING VISUALIZATION

Modern holistic practitioners have found that visualization is an excellent tool to aid the healing process. Dr Andrew Weil, a graduate of Harvard Medical School, has spent many years researching natural forms of healing. According to him, the visual cortex – provided it is not occupied with processing information received through the eyes – is able to connect mind and will through the control of the autonomic nervous system, and also elicit spontaneous healing. This statement has many implications. Dr Weil believes that the mechanisms for self-regeneration are embedded at every level of biological organization.

Visualizations, therefore, can be tailored to focus on any specific area of the body in need of healing, bringing into awareness the mind/body connection. For example, if there is a particular part of the body that is in need of attention, such as a stiff back, a sore ankle, a wound and so on, mental imagery can be used to influence the body's own healing potential.

It is best to start by centring yourself, which can be done by using one of the breathing techniques discussed earlier. Continue to focus on the breath and, as you slowly inhale, visualize the prana (life force) entering your body.

Once you feel completely relaxed, take a few deep breaths. As you breathe in, mentally direct the breath to any part of your body that may be in need of healing. Visualize the prana encircling and embracing that part of your body and giving forth positive healing energy. See and feel the area of concern ridding itself of the disease and visualize the disease being swept away. Let the disease flow out of the body when you exhale. Continue this process, allowing all the negativity to be replaced with the positive prana energy as you feel your body becoming whole and healthy. After a while, let go of all thought and drift into a meditative state for whatever period of time feels comfortable. When you have completed your meditation, gently open your eyes. Allow yourself some time to reflect on the meditation.

You may prefer to create imagery which is more personal. The best results are usually achieved when the visualization used to influence the body has particular meaning for the person in need.

Many years ago, I took part in a two-year healer's training programme which involved spending one weekend each month in the Berkshires in Massachusetts. When I was there during the winter months, I slept in a wonderful log house which had a wood burning stove as its only means of heat. One night as I got into bed, I felt the familiar scratching in my throat which always preceeded a full blown cold. Determined not to be ill the next day, but also not wanting to leave the cozy warm bed, I visualized myself getting out of bed and going into the kitchen and preparing a herbal tea blend, consisting of golden seal and several other herbs, that would help to heal the problem before it could fully manifest itself in the form of a cold. I felt the warming tea enter into my body and soothe my throat.

That night I had a wonderful sleep, and when I awoke the next day I felt absolutely fine, with more energy than I had had all week!

EMPATHIC MEDITATION

This is a technique in which empathy is employed, rather than visual imagination. The meditator tries to feel what it is like to be the object of the meditation. For example, rather than describing a tree to yourself, you *become* the tree.

Start by closing your eyes. Centre yourself, using one of the breathing techniques. When you are ready, imagine you are a tree. It may be a familiar one, or one that you mentally create. Feel your roots stretching into the earth.

Allow yourself to dwell for a while on what it is like to be a tree. What does your bark feel like? Do you have any leaves? Are there other trees around you? How do you feel? Only when you are ready,

gently open your eyes, and sit quietly for a few minutes as you settle back into normal consciousness. When you have completed your meditation, take a few minutes to examine how 'being a tree' compared with being yourself. You may be surprised at the number of similarities there are!

Becoming one with the tree enables you to know that it is possible to become one with any form.

Repeat the exercise occasionally, using other natural objects or forms. Become a cloud, a bird, a mountain, or whatever you fancy. You will soon develop greater appreciation and understanding for the universal oneness which we all seek.

MANDALAS AND YANTRAS (OTHER MEDITATION TOOLS)

Ancient aids to meditation from many traditions have been collected and adapted by modern meditators. Here are a few examples of how they are used today.

MANDALAS

Mandalas are complex arrangements of patterns or pictures. They are used in Hinduism and Buddhism, as well as in other traditions, to give expression to the infinite possibilities of the human subconscious. Exoterically, they are pictorial symbolic representations of the universe and its power, and can be conceived as places where the divinities reside. Esoterically, mandalas are mental diagrams, and can be used for meditation. An example of a mandala used as a tool in meditation is provided in Chapter Two, where the symbol for the Love theme, the rose, lends itself to a mandala representation. Mandalic depictions have varied from religion to religion, and tradition to tradition, yet their essential meanings and functions have remained the same from the earliest times.

The word mandala means 'circle', and in theory its simplest form is a circle, or a square with a central dot. But in practice, mandalas are elaborate designs, usually comprising a circular border,

enclosing further concentric circles which contain a square; the square itself is divided by diagonals, forming four triangles containing further circles or depictions of deities.

Using this basic schema, mandalas can be made to represent cities, gardens, palaces or even labyrinths. Whatever its form, a mandala is essentially a psychogram – a map of the inner condition of mind. The great Swiss psychologist, Carl Jung, used to quickly dash off a watercolour mandala before breakfast to see what sort of day he might expect!

You can use mandalas for meditation in two different ways. One is to spontaneously draw a set of concentric circles immediately after completing a period of single-point meditation *(see pages 64-5)*, something in the manner of Jung's method. The other, more usual way is either to use an existing mandalic form, or to draw or paint one yourself. The centre should be an empty, dark or light space, in which you can attempt to project a visualization of a deity that you find meaningful, or the image of a wise teacher or guru for whom you have a special affection. Or, you can use the mandalic form in a more abstract sense to meditate upon the nature of the Self: who is the 'I' behind the eye? What am

I when I take away all the superficial identifications with which I am associated, or think of as myself, in normal, daily life? What is it that is at the centre of the mandala?'

YANTRAS

Geometrically designed meditation figures with abstract mystical symbols are known as yantras. They are the prototype of the mandala, and have been found drawn or inscribed on metal, wood, skin, stone, paper or traced on a wall or the ground. A typical yantra consists of nine triangles – four apex up, five apex down – surrounded by several concentric circles. These elements are framed inside a square which has an 'entrance' on each side.

The openings in the square sides of a yantra are sometimes depicted as T-shaped portals. It is through these doors that the seeker symbolically enters on the journey from the earthly plane of matter to the internal sacred space.

Yantra is a Sanskrit word derived from the root yam, which means 'to sustain the energy found in a particular object or concept'.

Yantras are generally used as aids in religious meditative practices to help increase awareness. They represent a *temenos* (Greek for sacred enclosure), where the deity dwells.

There are similar forms of yantras in different religions, with multiple meanings for the symbols.

As well as the circle, a common yantra design is that of two interpenetrating triangles – one pointing up and the other pointing down – as depicted in the Star of David.

Traditionally, this shape symbolized the union of the male and female Hindu divinities – Shiva and Shakti, the union of opposites.

This union of the soul with God represents the goal of all religions.

One way the modern meditator might use a yantric diagram is to think of it as an expression of the forces or energies of creation, which generate the dynamics of the mind or spirit. While studying a yantric image, one can think of the descending triangle in the yantric diagram, for example, as the celestial or divine forces decending to meet the meditator, with the rising triangle representing the forces of nature raising the meditator's mind upwards towards the divine source.

The yantric diagram – whatever its design – can be thought of as a structure through which the dynamics of the mind can be ordered and focused for meditational purpose.

Adepts in the use of both mandalas and yantras soon progress to the stage where the image – or object of focus – becomes transformed into a living force within the mind.

GROUP MEDITATION

There are a number of benefits to be derived from meditating with a group of like-minded people. By openly discussing the meditation session afterwards, you not only gain from the insight of others, but you may also learn from their experiences. It is surprising, too, how often several people in a group will have a similar experience, particularly if the group has been meditating together for a while.

Most of the meditation techniques discussed in this kit can be used for group meditation. Some groups like to follow the same procedure each time they meet (usually once a week). Other groups may prefer experimenting with different techniques each session.

Meditation groups often have a healing circle at the end of their meditations. This consists of imagining a circle surrounded by white light. Each member, in turn or randomly as they feel inspired, can place people or objects inside the circle for healing. This is done by simply reciting the appropriate name, for instance, 'I place John in the light', while visualizing the person entering the circle. You need not be in a group to do this. You can include a variation of the healing circle at the end of your own meditation, if you wish.

MINI-MEDITATIONS

If you find yourself becoming tense, the relaxation benefits that you have obtained from meditating can be recalled at any time. Just having a two-minute mini-meditation can make a world of difference. All you need to do is find a quiet corner where you can sit down, close your eyes and compose yourself by using one of the breathing techniques discussed below.

You can even develop a mantra for just this purpose. When you are ready, simply take a few deep breaths and begin repeating your mantra, either silently or aloud – whichever is appropriate. You can keep your eyes open if necessary, which means that you can do this even if you are sitting on a bus with people all around you. Do take care, however, not to try a mini-meditation when your conscious attention is required, such as when you are driving your car or crossing the street!

Used appropriately, mini-meditations can be extremely useful. For example, tension can rise quickly while sitting in the dentist's waiting room. Rather than restlessly thumbing through one of the magazines or aimlessly reading an article for distraction, this can be the perfect time for a mini-meditation. A brief meditation ahead of a potentially nerve-wracking situation, where you need to remain focused and calm, such as a job interview or examination, can make all the difference.

ACQUIRING INSIGHT

Meditation is like any other activity: to do it well takes practice. It is important to remember that, even if you are never able to reach nirvana (few people are), allowing yourself the space and time for this practice can be a rewarding experience from your very first try.

When you start your meditation with one of the breathing techniques you have learned, the controlled breathing alone will help to centre you. You will feel calmer and clearer than when you started – even if you find you cannot fully block the normal chatter in your mind. By persevering, you will be able to expand your meditative state. It will happen; give yourself time.

The more you meditate, the more in tune with yourself you will become. Eventually, you may occasionally glimpse what the great poet Wordsworth called 'intimations of immortality' – spiritual insights – or even experience visionary episodes.

Above all, always remember that there are no hard-and-fast rules for meditation. What *The Meditation Kit* has given you is a set of guidelines, based on experience and research. Ultimately, you will find yourself beginning to acquire the insight and understanding you seek from your inner self.

At the end of your meditation, just prior to returning to full waking consciousness, you may want to recite (either out loud or internally) one or more affirmations. This can take the form of anything you wish to affirm to yourself – similar to a New Year resolution.

Here are some examples:

I shall maintain composure throughout the day.
I surround myself in a bubble of white light which only positive thoughts can penetrate.

I shall not smoke one cigarette all day.
I feel good about myself.
I will not argue with my boss. .... and so on.

As meditation has been increasingly practised in the West, our medical sciences have begun to realise that such deep calming can have beneficial effects on human behaviour, psychology and physiology. Chapter Five gives a brief overview of some of the main brain-mind-body connections that have been found, through sophisticated research, to be brought about by meditation.

CHAPTER FOUR

MEDITATION USING OTHER SENSES

Odors in and of themselves make myths possible.

GASTON BACHELARD

Our Western culture is basically visual. Objects and things in general are talked about in terms of how they are perceived – using terminology associated with the sense of sight. When someone describes an object that may not be directly visible, most people have no trouble 'seeing' it in their mind's eye – or at least their version of what is thought to look like the object being discussed. Even when an abstract concept is being explained, more often than not the reply will be, 'I see what you mean'. In reality, of course, what the person means can no more be seen than touched or tasted. But our society is so visual that seeing immediately becomes equated with understanding.

The second most valued sense in our Western society is hearing. We depend on it to help us communicate, and understand, what is happening directly around us and in the world in general. This is the reason why the tools provided in this kit rely primarily on vision and sound.

There are a number of meditation techniques that involve the other senses. By using some of them, discussed below, we can more fully appreciate – and bring into greater awareness – the value of all of our senses.

MANTRA MEDITATION

This is a technique in which sound is used, rather than sight or visualization. The term *mantra* is Sanskrit for thought form, or 'that which can change the mind'. By chanting or reciting a mantra, you can change the state of your mind completely: you are actually transforming the atmosphere and energy around you.

A mantra may consist of a single syllable or many verses. In its purest sense, a mantra represents primordial sound. Mantras, or sound vibrations, are used to help intensify and to complete the power of yantras. These vibrations are usually indicated on the yantra in the form of Sanskrit letters, and represent the spoken or written word. The mantra is believed to be vested with special spiritual power, and should not be thought of in terms of speech, but rather as a resonating wave of sound vibration.

Mantras have different purposes; for example, some can be used to help attain enlightenment while others are designed for protection. The mantra 'Om', shown here in its diagrammatical representation, is made up of five parts – each one corresponding to an element representing a basic principle of the universe. Each of these parts is individually known as a primary – or seed – mantra, because together they correspond to the quintessence of the powers of the universe.

You may use any mantra you wish for this meditation technique. It can be one of the mantras associated with the themes in the kit, or it can be any word as simple as 'love', or whatever other mantra that feels comfortable to you.

Your own voice is a meditational tool that you can bring to the meditative process. If you decide to use one of the mantras on the tape, play and replay the mantra of your choice until you can intone it yourself.

Sit in your meditative posture in a darkened room, and intone it audibly. Repeat this in a relaxed sequence several times. Try duplicating the sound silently within your mouth and throat. If using one of the mantras from the tape, you can make it resonate at the appropriate physical (chakra) level until you can virtually feel it vibrating at that point. For example, most fittingly, the 'Ah' of love will resonate in the heart area.

Gradually, you will learn to transmute the acoustic vibration of the mantra into a physically silent, internal mental vibration. This will take some practice, so do not become discouraged.

If you decide to make up your own mantra, choose any word or sound which you find pleasing. The word, or sound, should provoke a feeling of serenity within you when it is spoken. If you confine the use of your own mantra to meditation purposes only, it will be endowed with special meaning for you, and soon become a signal which, by its simple evocation, can almost produce the inner state that meditation brings. Be warned, however: using a negative word may well produce negative results.

Begin by getting into a comfortable position, and regulate your breath by using one of the breathing techniques you have learned. Read out the guided Mantra Meditation paragraph overleaf. If, as before, you wish to record it on your own tape, make sure you read slowly and carefully, pausing between each statement.

The Sufis felt that, 'when the heart begins to recite, the tongue should stop'. The goal of mantra meditation, then, is to overcome the static or constant chatter that occurs in the mind.

We must remember that every person has been endowed with a certain pitch, a natural note. No matter how unmusical we may feel our own voices to be, it is the sound nature has given us. The Sufi teacher Inayat Khan, father of Pir Vilayat Inayat Khan, points out that we try to define the focal range under labels such as suprano, tenor, baritone or base. We tend to limit what cannot be limited. 'There are as many voices as there are souls; they cannot be classified,' Inayat Khan has written.

He points out that one must first know how to breathe and then how to make a sound before one can utter a word.

Before you begin your Mantra Meditation, make yourself comfortable and relax your body, using one of the breathing techniques.

GUIDED MANTRA MEDITATION

 Spend five to ten minutes breathing deeply. As you inhale visualize glittering prana streaming into your body, making it glow within.

As you breathe out expel all your tensions and anxiety. Continue this combined breathing and visualization for at least five minutes: inhale prana, exhale stress. Think of your whole body as inhaling and exhaling. Continue until you feel completely relaxed and your mind flows in and out with each breath like the gentle roll of the tide on a smooth sandy shore.

Now, introduce your chosen mantra. With each inhalation and exhalation, mentally hear the sound of the mantra entering your body, much as you might hear the distant chime of church bells carried on a warm summer breeze. Continue with this until your breath and your mantra become as one.

Then let the sound of the mantra gradually fade away, but maintain your concentration on your breathe. Breathe fully and deeply. As the mantra fades away you are gently ushered to the shores of silence. You are entering a centre of peace, wisdom and bliss. The silence here contains all sound, much as a buzzing bee may be incased in amber. The more you focus, the more you hear the sound of silence, the more your mind becomes focused inwardly in a single-pointed manner.

You are merging into your essential nature which is in its essence a blissful and all-embracing peace.

The entire universe is contained in this vast ocean of ringing silence — no sound, no noise can disturb it once you have learned to tune to its frequency. Let the realization arise so powerfully within you that your essential nature, your true self, is identical with this Great Silence. Reside in this perfect state of tranquillity...

At this point remain silent for 10 minutes or stay quiet for as long as you feel comfortable. Then read on.

...Begin once more to focus on your breath and again mentally start to hear the sound of your mantra. Let it begin faintly, just shading the actual sound of your breathing. Mentally listen to the mantric sound strengthen and 'drive' your breathing. Allow the increasing sound of your mantra to draw you back to normal consciousness. Allow it to grow in power until gradually and softly at first you begin to audibly intone the mantra.

When your voice is fully uttering the mantric sound, you will have returned to normal consciousness. When you are ready, open your eyes.

(This meditation is based on one originally given by Swami Rama of the Himalayan Institute in Pennsylvania, USA.)

OTHER ACOUSTIC TECHNIQUES

In addition to mantras, other sounds are used in traditional meditation systems including bells, instruments, specific music and, of course, chanting. Sound is also a component in various trance-dancing techniques employed by some traditional peoples: the Native American 'long dance' in which the repetitive stomping sound enhances the hypnotic effect of the leg movements over many hours, and the !Kung of the Kalahari similarly use gourd rattles attached to the calves of their legs to heighten the trance-inducing effects of the repetitive motions of their protracted circular dances. Natural sounds are used in traditional meditation systems, such as rushing wind and roaring waterfalls at special places *(see pages 51-3)*.

Long drawn-out vibrating sounds have a stimulating effect on the mind, and possibly, on the physical brain. Singing or chanting produces a vibration in the vocal cords, even within bones and tissue, which feels like a mild, internal massage. Such sounds also create a kind of 'white noise' effect (a randomized sound effect that helps blot out intrusive sounds, having a similar psychological effect as total silence), which tunes out extraneous noise, helping to focus attention inwards. The repetition of chanting mantra can add a hypnotic effect – useful for meditation.

Tibetan Buddhists have mastered the art of sound associated with altering mind states most effectively; a very long horn emits a deep resonant note somewhat like a mantra, and is even more effective as a vehicle to transport the meditating mind. Their bells and percussive instruments may make a range of sounds somewhat discordant to the Western ear, but reproduce the sort of sounds one becomes accustomed to hearing internally when 'shifting gears' into higher states of consciousness (for example, in that transitionary phase of consciousness as one falls asleep). Powerful meditationally inducive sounds can be made with Tibetan bowls, which produce a resonant humming when a soft stick is rubbed around their rim. Rhythmic drumming also induces meditation. Rhythmic vibration, according to the ancient philosophies, is an intrinsic part of creation. The shamanic drum transported the meditator to another level of reality. The shaman beat the drum in a repetitive style, producing an undulating wave of sound rich in overtones.

FRAGRANCE MEDITATION

It is interesting that of our five senses, the sense of smell has the most direct connection to the brain. Yet it is probably the least understood. One reason may be because odours are so difficult to describe in words – and we live in a very verbal society.

Another reason was the influence of philosophers such as Plato and Aristotle, who felt that the sense of smell was not only less sophisticated, when compared to sight and hearing, but antisocial as well. In a similar fashion, Freud felt there was a direct connection between the decline of the sense of smell and the rise of civilization, and so in more modern times this sense came to be associated primarily with the animal kingdom.

It seems that schools of thought holding the mind and logic in high regard tended to denigrate olfaction, which eventually found a place in other areas, like poetry. For example, although the philosopher Bachelard placed great importance on smells, he did not feel that they belonged in the context of science. He felt that smells had special links with memory and the imagination. Modern researchers such as Dr Michael Kirk-Smith, of Ulster University, have been carrying out much work in this important area, studying the connection between memory and selected fragrances.

In many earlier cultures, however, perfume and incense were used as offerings to the deities, or to cast away evil spirits. Magicians of medieval times would anoint their bodies with special oils, which induced an altered state of consciousness in which visions were produced: the aim was to bring about a state of ecstasy. Basically, incense would have been used in meditation as a very effective aid in achieving the higher states of consciousness.

The average person is able to recognize as many as 10,000 different fragrances. The effect of smell is immediate, because the olfactory bulb is directly connected to the brain. A smell, therefore, can actually trigger an emotion before we are consciously aware of it. A familiar smell can be linked instantaneously to a past event – regardless of the present circumstance, which may be totally different from the environment that surrounded the origin of the smell. The fact that an odour can provoke memory is one of the aspects of the sense of smell that relates to meditation.

Scented candles and oils

We can work with fragrance in meditation in two distinct ways. One is using scented candles which are readily available. They add a different dimension to the starter candle provided in this kit, which you may have already used in the single-point meditations described above. Another way is to use a fragrance produced by vaporizing essential oils. The oils you choose to work with will depend on the atmosphere you desire to create, or the particular situation you want to work on.

Essential oils can have a powerful effect on our mental states (*see chart below*), which in turn will affect our physical health and vitality. For example, rose oil is considered to be the 'queen' of essential oils: in aromatherapy, it is often used for treating disorders of the female reproductive system, and it is believed to increase the production of semen.

The theme of Love
The scent of roses is extremely uplifting, and burning rose essential oil in a fragrancer is an effective anti-depressant. Rose is also known as an aphrodisiac. Indeed, the Romans would sprinkle rose petals on the bridal bed. These qualities make rose oil an excellent scent to use when meditating on the theme of Love.

The theme of Peace
Frankincense has been recognized as a powerful influence on the mind and has been used in ritual ceremonies for thousands of years. (Frankincense was such a precious commodity in ancient times that wars were fought for its possession!) The inhalation of frankincense is said to heighten spiritual awareness, deepening the religious or magical experience obtained from the ritual act. It has a calming effect, and is one of the most popular oils used in association with meditation as it helps to

FRAGRANCE AND THEME

You may want to develop an association between a particular fragrance and one of the four themes discussed in this kit. Below are some suggested oils to use with the themes.

Love Rose

Peace Frankincense

Balance Geranium

Transformation Cypress

deepen and slow the rate of breath. Frankincense is an ideal fragrance to use when meditating on the theme of Peace because of these qualities.

The theme of Balance

The relaxing, warming and balancing qualities of geranium make it the perfect fragrance to use when meditating on the theme of Balance. The inhalation of geranium has a calming effect on the body and mind. Small amounts of the oil of geranium are often used in essential oil blends as it helps to 'bring them together'.

The theme of Transformation

Cypress (*Cupressus sempervirens*) is the essential oil suggested for meditating on the theme of Transformation. The Latin word *sempervirens* means evergreen, and refers to the leaves of the tree.

The Egyptians dedicated the cypress tree to their gods of death and the afterworld as they believed the tree was connected with the afterlife.

Cypress trees have since been traditionally planted in cemeteries for thousands of years. Thus the essential oil of cypress is always recommended for use in times of transition.

USING OILS AND FRAGRANCE

Whatever oil or fragrance you may choose to work with, the most important thing is that you find the smell pleasing.

Whether you use scented candles or essential oils to meditate, it is best to have the fragrance dispersed in the room for your first few meditations. As you are focusing on your chosen theme, the background scent will become part of your mental connection with the theme.

Once the fragrance penetrates the room, you can begin your meditation, using one of the deep breathing exercises described in your kit. If you have not yet tried one of those, just close your eyes and allow yourself to completely relax by breathing deeply.

Use a fragrancer or, if you do not have a fragrancer to hand, place several drops of the oil fragrance on a ball of cottonwool or a spare piece of cloth, which you hold in your cupped hands. Inhale deeply as you shut your eyes.

Each time you inhale, focus exclusively on the fragrance, and allow the scent to take you on a journey of discovery. When you feel ready – it will probably take you about fifteen minutes – gently open your eyes. A most effective method of recentring when you find yourself in a stressful situation is to carry the fragrance.

SUGGESTED ESSENTIAL OILS TO USE FOR MEDITATION

A fragrant room: a pleasant scent present in a room during meditation can be a positive experience, whether or not used as a focal point to the meditation. For instance, incense cones or joss sticks are often burnt before or during meditation – although some people may find their strong scent too overpowering.

• *The oil(s) you choose will depend on the mood or situation you want to work with.*
• *Remember that you can use the oils individually or blend two together.*
• *It is important that you find the smell pleasing.*
• *You will soon associate the scent with your chosen theme.*
• *You can also carry the fragrance with you; using it for just a few minutes will make a difference.*

MOOD	OIL
Tension	lavender, ylang ylang, geranium
Lethargy	orange, peppermint, rosemary
Anxiety	lavender, neroli, sandalwood
Irritability	bergamot FCF, chamomile, rose
Overall stress	lavender, sandalwood, chamomile
Uplifting/stimulating	melissa, mandarin, rosemary

Note: Frankincense is excellent to use for a general meditation on you: you will be able to recall the theme you are working with by just smelling the scent. Just a few minutes alone with your fragrance can usually do the trick.

You can also use scent with meditation by associating it with the theme image card just before going to sleep. As you fall into sleep, try to visualize the image you have been studying, and the scent will travel with you into the realm of dreams.

You may even want to ask yourself, and explore, the question: 'Were any of my memory associations triggered by this fragrance?' If there were none, examine how the fragrance made you feel. For example, if the fragrance made you feel calm, you may want to include it again as part of your meditation when you have had a particularly stressful day.

In this way, you are beginning to build your own fragrance-memory connections by conditioning yourself to a fragrance association.

Fragrance and memory

Another, more individual way of working with fragrance in meditation depends on your own personal memory. Think of a fragrance that has a pleasant association for you. It will need to be one that you can easily obtain – like a perfume you can buy, or one that you can recreate, such as the smell of freshly brewed coffee.

Incorporate the fragrance in the room. If it is a perfume, it can be sprayed, or simply put onto a tissue that you inhale. Depending on the fragrance you choose, you may find that you do have to be a little creative.

The aim is to start your meditation by gently closing your eyes and inhaling the fragrance, in the same way as indicated in the previous exercise. Breathe in the fragrance and allow your mind to explore whatever is triggered by the scent. When you are ready, gently open your eyes.

You may be surprised to find that you remembered things associated with the fragrance which you had not thought about for a long time – that until now were buried deep within your own memory.

This type of meditation may also be useful to help you understand why you feel a particular way about a fragrance. For example, a friend had a strong dislike for frankincense, which happens to be one of the essential oils used for meditation. By burning some frankincense oil in a burner during a meditation, the friend was able to remember what made him dislike it: when he was a child, he did not like to go to church because it meant that he had to sit quietly for what seemed like an endless period of time. Understandably, for a young child who would rather be outside running and playing with his friends, sitting in church for long periods of time was extremely unpleasant. Part of the church ceremony included the burning of frankincense. Because the fragrance was associated with unpleasant experiences in his mind, he still found the odour unpleasant when he smelled it again many years later. Once this association was understood, it no longer bothered him.

TOUCH MEDITATION

A highly polished stone, small enough to fit comfortably in the palm of your hand, is a perfect focus for the practice of touch meditation. Allow yourself to rotate the stone through your fingers, exchanging it from one hand to the other, feeling its smooth texture.

In fact, any small, smooth-surfaced object can be used in this way. You may already have such small objects that you have collected and cherish, from stones you have found on the beach and chestnuts to small carved artefacts.

The use of a chaplet of beads for recording the number of prayers recited seems to date back to the Egyptian anchorites. Worry beads, which have their origin in the Middle East and are used to reduce stress, can also be used in meditation. Rosary beads are used as a focus for prayer in the Catholic religion.

Chinese exercise balls, too, are effective for relaxation and focusing attention for meditation. They have the added benefit of stimulating the acupuncture points on the hand.

According to traditional Chinese medical theory, there are points on our fingers which are linked, by means of channels, to the various major organs in our body. Vital energy is said to flow through these channels. By rotating the Chinese exercise balls in the palms of your hands with your fingers, the acupuncture points are thus stimulated, resulting in an unimpeded flow of blood and vital energy throughout the body.

By focusing on this exercise, therefore, you will not only quieten the mind – preparing it for meditation – but you will also benefit from strengthening your muscle tone, and positively affecting other parts of your body as well.

Another method for touch meditation is actually a form of psychometry – the ability to divine factual information from an object, or about a person associated with the object.

Hold a ring or other small object in the palm of your hand, and focus your attention entirely on that object.

How to practise touch meditation

Gently close your eyes, and use one of the breathing techniques.

Then allow yourself to float into a state of calm, while still focusing on the object in your hand. Note how it feels, and any other reactions that you may have. You may be surprised at the thoughts that enter your mind.

Gently allow the process to continue, until you are ready to open your eyes and return to normal consciousness.

You may want to discuss the images that came into your mind during your meditation with the owner of the object you held, to discover whether you picked up any accurate information that was previously unknown to you.

CHAPTER FIVE

MEDITATION, SCIENCE AND PSYCHOLOGY

The mind modulates what goes on in the body.

THOMAS DELBANCO

Traditionally, the vocation of both meditation and medicine has always been to heal. In contrast to meditation, however, modern allopathic (conventional) medicine deals only with the body and teaches us to cure the symptom, rather than try to determine the cause.

Fortunately, the tide is turning: there is now increasing evidence that mind and body are closely related, and that consequently, whatever is done to or for the one will have a direct effect on the other.

The interest in meditation as a tool for relaxation and healing has grown in modern society since it was discovered that science was able to monitor brainwaves. Known as biofeedback, this technique has helped greatly to give meditation the credentials it needed to be regarded as an acceptable and useful form of modern practice.

It was the electroencephalograph (EEG) which made this possible. The EEG is an instrument which measures the electrical activity of the brain and records it in graphform, or electroencephalogram. In response to signals given out by the monitoring EEG machine, the subject learns to modify electrical activity in the brain (and in other areas, such as skin resistance).

Ultimately, the subject is able to produce the desired brain wave pattern on command.

MEDITATION AND SCIENCE

Many of today's meditators are essentially interested in the physical and mental benefits of what they call 'the relaxation response,' and tend to consider meditation as a way of obtaining an even deeper state of relaxation than the sleep state. There is nothing wrong in using meditation in this way, of course, but it does not constitute the fullest nor the most profound use of the method: the less obvious psychospiritual aspects of meditation are ignored.

In the mid 1970s, Dr Herbert Benson, a Harvard University cardiologist, provided the first laboratory proof that metabolism can be lowered as a result of meditation. In association with several colleagues, Benson conducted an experiment which compared patients who meditate with others who do not, checking the progress of each at the point when they were discharged.

The study revealed that the psychiatric condition of those who meditated had improved significantly more than in the case of the non-meditators. In addition, it was noted that the meditating patients often required lighter dosages of tranquillizers. And some patients who had normally experienced difficulty in sleeping found that they were able to sleep better when they meditated — allowing them to significantly reduce or eliminate sleep-inducing medication.

Benson believed that four basic elements are required in order to be able to achieve a beneficial relaxation response: (i) a quiet environment; (ii) a comfortable position so that minimum muscle work is required (but not lying down, to avoid the possibility of falling asleep); (iii) use of a technique, verbal or visual, to help change the mind from its normal, logical, externally oriented thought processes, to the internally oriented mental state required to facilitate the relaxation response; (iv) a passive attitude – in other words, any distracting thoughts that may occur must be ignored, and the attention brought back to the technique being used. Interestingly, these are the guidelines that have traditionally been recommended for meditation practice.

MONITORING TECHNIQUES

Modern techniques teach us how to control our bodily and mental functions with the aid of a visual – or auditory – display of our own brain waves, blood pressure, muscle tension, and so on. The basic principle is, that if you can become aware of what takes place in the body below the usual threshold of your waking consciousness, you can learn to control it.

Biofeedback

With the initial help of biofeedback instrumentation, it is easy to learn how to control your own brain/mind states. For example, alpha rhythms (waves of about 8-10 cycles per second) are normally produced without your being consciously aware of it. One way of deliberately producing alpha rhythms is through meditation.

By demonstrating to you how quickly to induce alpha brainwaves, you can speed up your progress in meditation. In short, biofeedback allows a person to become more immediately conscious of the links between the state of the mind and brain activity, and how to control that relationship.

Galvanic skin response

Another technique is the galvanic skin response, which can be used to measure stress. Electrodes are placed on the skin surface, and a mild electric current is conducted across the skin. In a calm state, the skin normally resists the electric current. In a state of stress or anxiety, however, skin resistance drops, allowing an electric current to flow easily across.

On the other hand, tests have shown that skin resistance often rises during meditation. Psychologist David Orme-Johnson, of the University of Texas, considered the question: 'Does regular meditation change the way a person deals with stress?' His basic hypothesis was that, under stress conditions, meditators have a greater capacity to recover than non-meditators.

He tested that theory by setting up two groups, one of meditators and the other non-meditators. A loud drilling noise was sounded intermittently, and the skin resistance of every subject was tested on each occasion. Orme-Johnson wanted to see how long it would take the subjects to get used to the sound, and if meditation made a difference. The answer was to be found at the point when the skin no longer reacted to the sound.

For the meditators, this point was reached when the sound was heard for the eleventh time. The non-meditators, however, continued to react each time the sound was repeated – forty times in all. The research went on to investigate this area by a number of other significant experiments. One in particular was quite intriguing. The non-meditators from previous experiments were given instruction in TM. Within several weeks after learning and practising the technique, their galvanic skin response scores were almost as low as those of the long-term meditators.

HOW DOES MEDITATION WORK?

The human brain is divided into two hemispheres, the left being the dominant half of the brain – at least in our Western societies – dealing with logical thought, sequential analysis and speech. The right hemisphere of the brain is capable of recognizing individual people, reading maps, and enjoying art and music. (Interestingly, although it is the left side of the brain which controls speech, it is the right side of the brain that allows us to sing!)

It has been shown that communication between the two halves of the brain can be accomplished in

BRAIN-BODY ASSOCIATIONS

Different activities of the body are controlled by different areas of the mind

RIGHT HEMISPHERE

Controls left side of the body: space perception, intuition, musical awareness, artistic awareness.

LEFT HEMISPHERE

Controls right side of the body: verbal activity, logic, sequential thinking, practical thinking.

Research has shown that communication between the two hemispheres can be achieved by meditation.

meditation, thus creating a balance between right and left brain.

Research carried out in 1975 by Dr Bernard Glueck, at the Institute of Living in Hartford, Connecticut, demonstrated that people practising TM showed an increased synchrony between the left and the right sides of the brain. Glueck compared the effects of TM to taking intravenous Valium – which has the effect of slowing down the dominant alpha rhythm.

BRAIN RHYTHMS

Brain rhythms fall into four basic classifications: beta, alpha, theta, and delta, and are characterized by their frequency *(see chart below)*. As mentioned previously, people normally produce alpha rhythms without being consciously aware of it. But one way of deliberately producing alpha rhythms is through meditation.

We are often unaware of what can initiate a stressful situation. By recording brain signals, it is possible to discover what is happening exactly at the point when alpha rhythms cease. If we can become aware of what are the causes that underlie stress in our lives, we can work to help eliminate it from happening.

Meditation has a direct effect on the pattern of electrical waves in the brain, producing a strong calming sequence of alpha rhythms (state of calm, detached awareness) and theta rhythms (dreamlike) to develop. Dr Keith Wallace and his colleagues, at the Harvard Medical School, found these effects to be quite different from the physiological changes that can be observed when simply sitting quietly, or during actual sleep. In 1971, they described meditation as 'an alert, hypometabolic state' and 'a fourth major state of consciousness,' finding that it can result in a deeper

BRAIN RHYTHMS

	BETA (13–30 Hz)	normal waking state associated with daily activity with focus on the outside world
	ALPHA (8–13 Hz)	state of dream or empty mind
	THETA (4–7 Hz)	dreamlike state usually just prior to sleep, deep meditation
	DELTA (0.5–4 Hz)	deep sleep, higher levels of conciousness

state of relaxation than sleep, as indicated by greater reductions in the metabolic rate.

Because it can record brainwave activities – showing when (or if) a person is actually in a state of meditation – some believe that biofeedback is a good way for beginners to learn how to meditate. Others, however, believe that there is no intrinsic connection between a neurological state of enhanced occipital alpha (representing eye muscle activity rather than brainwaves) and a meditative state of consciousness.

Interestingly, an abundance of alpha waves, followed by theta waves, are often present in the brain wave tracings of experienced meditators during their meditation. For example, Zen monks show an ability to remain 'in theta' for extended periods of time without actually falling asleep.

It does not follow, however, that by bringing about certain changes in brain wave patterns we can instantly reach nirvana. There is more to meditation than just a shift in brain wave patterning!

Neurologist J. P. Banquet carried out some experiments with TM meditators which indicated that the most interesting aspect of the meditator's brain activity may not be one specific wave or pattern of waves, but the unusual evenness and rhythmicity of whichever wave form is occurring – the tendency for all areas of the brain to harmonize and pulsate together during meditation. Specifically, the meditators were asked to push a button when they entered a new stage of meditation – with a different signal for each of five types of meditative experience.

The records revealed that, when four of the advanced meditators indicated that they were either in deep meditation or pure awareness, the brain wave trace showed that the alpha wave pattern shifted to a fast beta wave at the precise moment the button was pushed. Fast beta is a wave form typical of the active, waking state. However, the beta indicated was different from the usual waking beta in that it was totally 'in phase': the recordings from different areas of the brain were synchronized. Ordinarily, waking state beta waves are uneven and unpredictable.

A clue to this synchronization effect may be gleaned from yogic rhythmic breathing. When this is practised properly, it is said that the whole system catches the vibration and becomes in harmony with the will – which is the explanation given by the yogis for their ability to increase the circulation in any part of their body, or direct an increased current of nerve force to any organ to strengthen and stimulate it. Indeed, a simple note on a violin, if sounded repeatedly and in constant rhythm, can project vibrations which in time can actually destroy a bridge. And a regiment of soldiers will 'break step' when marching across a bridge, in case the vibration that is produced by the synchronous marching might have the same disastrous effect.

Psychologist Lester Fehmi developed 'open focus' meditation as a result of experiments with a number of methods.

His subjects were connected to an EEG unit, to observe the effect of individual suggestions on each subject's brainwaves. As a result, he was able to determine which produced the most dramatic effects. Open focus – basically a guided-imagery meditation – attempts to simulate a Zen-type experience of oneness with the surrounding environment. Parapsychologists too, are looking at brain waves associated with meditation: they believe that extrasensory perception (ESP) may be related to alpha waves, which dominate in meditation. Rhea White, of the American Society for Psychical Research, correlated the methods used by ESP percipients to bring their impressions into consciousness with meditation procedures. People who have a gift for ESP tend to have a feeling of oneness with their surroundings – something that the meditator strives for.

MEDITATION AND PHYSIOLOGY

Orthodox medicine is becoming aware of the extraordinary physiological benefits that meditation can bring. Some of these benefits include reduction of tension, and the actual disappearance of many psychosomatic ailments which are primarily related to states of overarousal – stress-related symptoms such as high blood pressure, insomnia and bad digestion. It has been shown that modern-day problems, for instance anxiety, strain, over-aggressiveness, even heart beat and respiratory levels, can all significantly be decreased.

Meditation also seems to enhance muscle tone and maintain proper blood cortisone levels. The overriding reason is that meditation promotes relaxation, and when the body is relaxed, reduction of tension and its attendant physiological markers becomes possible. The added benefit of meditation is a simultaneous increase in general energy and overall health.

Leon Chaitow, Doctor of Osteopathy and Natural Medicine and a British writer on alternative approaches, considers meditation to be 'the ultimate mental detoxification tool'.

The use of visualization, or guided-imagery meditation, has been shown to be a positive tool in helping to relieve pain and in some cases it has actually cured illness.

And by practising meditation on a regular basis, stress can be avoided altogether. Various meditation practices are being used as a complementary approach alongside conventional medical techniques in some hospitals, as well as being taught in medical schools.

A most fascinating paper, published in *The Anthropology of Consciousness Journal* in 1995 by Richard J. Castillo, of the Division of Social Sciences at the University of Hawaii, shows that physiological changes associated with meditation have been observed in heart rate, the redistribution of blood flow, lowering of blood pressure, and changes in blood chemistry – including changes in levels of adrenal hormones, amino acids and phenylalanine, plasma prolactin and growth hormone, lactate, serotonin, white blood cells, red blood cell metabolism and cholesterol.

The implications are that the practice of meditation can provoke dramatic and positive effects on the overall physiology.

Early studies in the field of psychoimmunology have indicated that strong emotions, such as depression or feelings of loss, can provoke an immune system response.

In addition, Joan Borysenko, of the Beth Israel Hospital in Boston, says that meditation and relaxation directly affect natural killer cells and hydrocortisone levels of the immune system. Meditation has also been shown to have a positive effect on patients with diabetes, ultimately lowering their need for insulin.

MEDITATION AND HORMONES

Interesting research is being carried out in a number of areas by mainstream orthodox professionals. For example, melatonin (a neurohormone that works both as a hormone and as a neurochemical) has been shown to induce drowsiness, and, when orally ingested, to alter the normal rhythms of sleep and waking state.

Melatonin is considered to be a major link between the pineal gland, where it is produced and primarily secreted, and other hormonal glands and systems in the body. The pineal gland is a small, cone-shaped organ, located in the centre of the brain near the hypothalamus and pituitary gland; for a long time, it was thought by modern science to have no function. However, Eastern mystics, believed that the pineal gland, known as 'the third eye' or 'seat of the soul', was directly involved with meditation and clairvoyance.

Melatonin tablets are sometimes used to combat jet-lag by resetting the biological clock. Italian physician Paolo Lissoni has obtained positive results by giving cancer patients – with advanced tumours and a life expectancy of less than six months – 40mg doses of melatonin daily.

Two preliminary studies reported in 1996, one conducted at the University of Massachusetts Medical Center, the other a Saybrook Institute doctoral study conducted at the University of Western Ontario Research Park, suggest that there is a link between meditative practice and an increase in the supply of melatonin. This was established by measuring the major melatonin metabolite (6-sulphatoxy-melatonin) in urine. The study in Massachusetts recorded the difference between the levels of melatonin in eight experienced meditators versus a control group of the same number of non-meditators: a higher level of melatonin was found in the meditators.

In the Saybrook study, fifteen meditators were studied, twelve of whom were healthy and three suffered with cancer. Ranjie Singh, who conducted the study, was interested to see if a combination of mantra, visualization and special breathing techniques which induced deep meditation, could stimulate the pineal gland, as measured by the melatonin. The study showed that differences in urinary levels of melatonin, before and after the practice of these techniques, showed increases in melatonin which varied between 7 and 1,000 percent. Singh said that the naturally produced melatonin levels were actually higher than if a 5mg melatonin tablet had been orally ingested.

As a result of the trials with melatonin in the United States, a long-term study of the effect of meditation on women in the early stages of breast cancer is underway. No doubt further in-depth research in this area is needed.

A note of caution here – the research is studying levels of naturally produced melatonin. While it is true that melatonin tablets are readily available over the counter in the United States, there is concern that there has not been enough research to suggest what the long-term effects might be as a result of taking melatonin on a regular basis, for purposes other than what might be prescribed for specific indications. In Britain, all hormones are classified as drugs. In 1994 the Medicines Control Agency agreed to consider granting a licence for the sale of melatonin if manufacturers can prove its safety and efficacy. But this is not yet the case.

No doubt it is easier to carry out research dealing with physiological changes than with reported psychological benefits of meditation. Some tests, however, seem to indicate that, after meditation, subjects have done better on problems requiring logical thinking than they did after a period of normal rest. The significance of these results, and of similar tests, is that the degree of relaxation reached as a result of meditation seems to have had an important role to play: the deeper the state of relaxation the meditator is able to achieve, the greater the immediate benefits obtained from activities performed directly after meditation.

MEDITATION AND BRAIN CELLS

In the early 1960s, the anthropologist A. Neher suggested that rhythmic drumming could affect mind states because the repetitive sound induced 'auditory driving' in the brain. This means that the rhythmic auditory stimulation provided by the drumming imposes a synchronized firing pattern on brain cells, distinct from the normal, more randomized discharging of the cells. It is exceptionally interesting to note that fasting increases the susceptibility of the brain to the driving influences of rhythmic stimulation.

Auditory driving facilitates what is termed high-voltage hypersynchrony in the low alpha or theta brainwave frequencies, which tend to be the ones most dominant during meditation. A study conducted in 1990 by M.C. Maxfield backs this up to a certain extent by showing that a driving effect was notable in the theta range, among normal adult subjects.

Researcher Andrija Puharich, an American neurologist well known for his study of extrasensory perception, analysed the acoustic properties of a drum identical to the type used in ritual practices by the shaman of the Tungus people, a tribe from Siberia.

Frequency analysis of recordings made from the sound of the drum revealed a continuous sonic output maintained at about 35 decibels, with peak outputs marking each drumbeat. The drumbeats provided the tempo, energy and frequencies stimulating the shaman in the early stages of the ritual. It seems that the shaman sets the rhythm of his entire organism by this stimulation, enhanced by synchronized breathing. As the ritual progresses the tempo increases, thereby affecting the temporal lobes in the shaman's brain and causing the sort of driving effect suggested by Neher.

To try and understand what effects various rhythms might have on the listener, a study using undergraduates was conducted at Princeton University, in 1974, to see how they responded to various types of syncopated (two-beat) rhythms played on a drum. The speed-regulated drumbeats were recorded on tape. Five speeds were recorded, some being close to that of the normal heart beat, others quite different. The results were strongly in favour of speeds that were close to the normal heart-beat range – 60-72 beats per minute; the participants felt relaxed. Beats outside this range made them feel tense and anxious.

The results of this study provide some insight into the deeply calming effects that can be obtained by meditation. Most Eastern practices place great emphasis on breathing when entering into meditation. In addition, most people find that when repeating their mantra it naturally links with the rhythm of their breath.

MEDITATION AND PSYCHOLOGY

Some researchers consider meditation to be a unique state, which differs from the waking or the sleeping states but which also contains some of the attributes of each.

In other words, in the course of meditation the body seems to enter a state of complete relaxation similar to that of sleep, yet the mind remains alert as in the waking state.

Other research indicates that meditation may be a prolonged hypnogogic (pre-sleep) state, called by the Tantrics – followers of a Tibetan doctrine inspired by Buddhism (*see Appendix*) – 'the fourth state of consciousness'.

Dr Andreas Mavromatis, who published an in-depth study of the hypnogogic state in his book, *Hypnogogia*, in 1987, views it as the juncture point between the sleeping, dreaming and waking.

MANTRA MEDITATION AND MOODS
The Rishi mystics (a Hindu term meaning inspired sage or poet) understood the scientific quality of sound, which early man only sensed. The most important, or valuable, aspect of the music of ancient peoples, was that they distinguished between the different affective aspects of sound, and thereby came to realize that certain ways of expressing tone and rhythm produced stronger emotion, or motivated action. They also discov-

ered that a certain use of time and rhythm brought about greater equilibrium and greater poise.

After development and many years of practice, this knowledge turned into a special psychological science, or art, which was called mantra yoga.

Although an archaic science, mantra yoga took sound into different realms, for it was soon realized that sound is an energy vibration: the use of certain types of music to stimulate plant growth, for example, is no longer viewed merely as a pleasant myth. It was also understood that certain sound vibrations can directly affect specific parts of the human body. In a less subtle way, modern technology has rediscovered this fact: the NASA, for instance, has conducted extensive acoustic surveys and found that certain sonic frequencies can affect various parts of the body, and have both physiological and psychological effects. These frequencies 'open' the areas they relate to, and stimulate them into positive physical and mental activity. 'What we call matter or substance, and all that does not seem to speak or sound, is in reality all vibration', stated the Sufi sage, Inayat Khan.

The Eastern teachers were able to sense the physical and psychological needs of their disciples intuitively. They would then choose a sound vibration, or mantra, that would benefit the spiritual and physical wellbeing of the disciple. After a period of time, which could be short or long depending on the disciple's innate ability, the mantra would produce an almost alchemical change in the individual.

The idea that specific mantras have specific effects makes sense when you think how different sounds will produce certain responses. When you run your fingernails down a blackboard, for instance, it produces a particular reaction in the body. In fact, just thinking about it can actually produce the same body sensation! Since specific sounds elicit specific responses, it then logically follows that by repeating one particular sound over and over, either aloud or silently, a certain effect will be produced that will be related to the sound. If you change the sound, the effect of that sound should also change accordingly.

In 1976, an experiment was carried out at Princeton University, by researchers Douglas Moltz and Patricia Carrington, to formally investigate the effects of word sounds on mood. They chose, at random, single-syllable sounds which had no particular meaning in the English language. A total of fifteen such 'nonsense syllables' were selected, five which seemed to be very soothing, another five which were rather jarring and a further five which conveyed a neutral effect. The list of sounds was given to 100 subjects, who were asked to mentally repeat each sound and rate it on a seven-point graded scale which ranged from 'extremely soothing' to 'extremely jarring'. As there was a high percentage of agreement, it was easy to select three sounds, one from each group.

The three selected sounds were then presented to a group of thirty students, none of whom had ever meditated. They were asked to repeat each of the sounds silently for a period of five minutes. After the end of each five-minute period, they were requested to describe their mood while repeating the particular sound, by using one or more of a list of adjectives indicated on a checklist. (It should be noted that before being given the first sound, the students had been asked to mark the adjectives that best described their mood just prior to the start of the experiment.) The object was to see if different word-sounds had different effects on mood, thereby testing the claim of the meditative traditions – that particular mantras have particular effects.

The three sounds chosen were 'lõm', 'noi', and 'grik'. The results showed that the repetition of the sound 'lõm' caused a significant decrease in anger and hostility, while 'grik' had the opposite effect, causing an angry and irritable mood to increase significantly. However, it was discovered that repeating the word 'grik' also caused a decrease in depression and dejection. What is of interest here is that, according to a well-known clinical observation, when a depressed person feels anger at something or someone outside him or herself, the depression often disappears.

There were other findings as well. Both the sounds 'lõm' and 'noi' had positive effects on feelings of fatigue. And of the three sounds, 'noi' was the only one which had the effect of reducing tension and anxiety. In short, this preliminary study demonstrated what the earlier cultures who practised mantra already knew – sound can affect human mood.

When you look closely at various traditional mantra sounds, you will note that most of them end in a resonant nasal sound, such as 'n', 'm' or 'ng'. The best-known mantra, 'om', is a case in point. These sounds seem to reverberate internally. Of course we must take into account any mental associations we may have for a particular word. These associations are usually individual, although certain sounds carry a universal meaning.

SOME PSYCHOLOGICAL BENEFITS OF MEDITATION

Based on many psychological studies that have been carried out to date (too many to adequately discuss here), the list of activities that meditation seems to enhance include: an anti-addictive effect on drug, alcohol and cigarette abuse; the ability to solve mathematical problems; increase in academic performance among college students; better job performance and satisfaction; positive effect on interpersonal relationships; increased self-esteem; cure or control of a number of diseases.

In the early 1980s, the Harvard Medical School conducted studies which concluded that long-term meditation can lead to new perceptual/cognitive states.

In other words, this means that people who have been meditating for a long time seem to have more refined mental control and less emotional involvement with their thoughts, along with a greater discriminative capacity.

It was felt that meditation practice changes information processing in fundamental and potentially permanent ways – providing the meditators with much greater depth of perception and less emotional attachment. This can be particularly important if you live, or work, in an environment where the people closest to you are ill or have a poor attitude. The attitudes of those whom you share your environment with can all too easily 'rub off' on you, without your being aware of it. Attitude can be infectious!

Nature's way

Scientists will certainly be debating on how meditation works for some time to come: it is understandably difficult for scientists to understand states of consciousness which they have not personally experienced.

But there is no doubt that meditation for Western society is more than just a passing phase. This will become ever more true as our mainstream way of life becomes increasingly fraught and stress-filled.

It is already the case that people who resort to psychological counselling because of dysfunctions resulting from physical stress and anxieties, engendered by the lifestyles to which we are so prone today, are too often prescribed 'happy pills' – a chemical fix for the problem. Not only does this tend to mask real problems rather than trying to solve them, but it can also lead to drug dependency, and further complications, as has been exemplified by the recent controversies surrounding the drug Prozac. Meditation offers nature's way of dealing with such difficulties.

It should not be overlooked that meditation can at the same time address that great spiritual vacuum that is growing within all of our modern industrial societies.

Meditation is truly a powerful, natural approach to the ills that beset mind, body and spirit. The natural approach – meditation – is one that is still insufficiently used. It is hoped that this book and kit can provide the first steps for many more people along the road of healing and enlightenment that meditation represents.

THE EVOLUTION OF MEDITATION TECHNIQUES

We in the West do not have to give up our own proven resources in order to appropriate the best another culture has to offer; here may well be the crucible where East meets West to forge a new source of healing.

BILL MOYERS

Meditation can be placed within a vast context of human experience with the secrets of the mind – an experience which goes back through untold generations, independent of race, colour, age and sex. It has been a psycho-spiritual tool to a greater or lesser extent in most cultures from the beginning of time. The techniques employed in the striving for mystical enlightenment may vary widely, and the results interpreted differently, yet the ultimate experience remains the same: the direct experience of God. Although in history many mystics were associated with a particular religion, there exists a fundamental difference between religion and mysticism. Both are concerned with the sacred realm; but while most religions associate the sacred with a particular deity, mysticism correlates the sacred with the deep, unreconized 'real self' of each individual.

A number of Eastern meditation systems have taken root in the West, aided and abetted by the tremendous interest in Eastern spiritual traditions that flowered in the 1960s. But whereas Eastern religions view meditation as a sort of spiritual commitment, most people in the West approach meditation in a more compartmentalized way, treating it on a par with physical exercise, healing practices or psychotherapy.

The Western approach also has the advantage of 'hindsight vision' – we are in the fortunate position of being able to review different systems of meditation from all times and places, perhaps even combining several different techniques and systems – which cannot be done within the confinement of a single, belief-oriented tradition.

SHAMANISM

Perhaps the earliest form of meditation was developed in shamanism, which has been present in almost every society from early times, and still exists to some extent. The shaman was the tribal healer, entertainer and mystic, who acted as intermediary between the members of the tribe and the visionary world of the ancestors and spirits. He or she would go into a trance to obtain knowledge, information, or healing power, in the interests of the tribe. As a consequence, the shaman was a figure of supernatural powers. The influence of the shaman can be traced even in the world's great religions.

Shamanism still survives in some societies today. For example, the !Kung Bushmen of the Kalahari desert, in South Africa, still practise a technique, known as trance dancing, which is part of their approach to healing. They will have a dance whenever it seems necessary, and it is always a group event.

These dances are usually started in the early evening by the women, who sit around the fire, singing and rhythmically clapping their hands. The men and some women then start dancing around the singers. After a very prolonged period of dancing – the entire ritual usually lasts until morning – some of the dancers begin to shake violently, as though their whole body was in convulsion and in much pain. This is known as kia, which is activated by an energy that the !Kung call n/um. The Bushmen believe that n/um resides in the pit of the stomach and at the base of the spine.

As the dance progresses, the spiritual potency, or energy, turns into heat, and the dancers begin to sweat profusely. The n/um rises up the spine to a point approximately at the base of the skull, at which moment kia results. The experience of kia is a necessary pre-requisite for healing. Similarly, one of the rituals of Native Americans is the 'long dance', in which participants dance all night and sometimes all day in a special location. Dancing consists of foot-stomping, which helps to induce a state of trance. Such tribal peoples made use of other various aids to trance induction. For instance, the sound of a ritual drum, with its persistent beat, is able to produce a state of trance. The glow and flicker of a fire can be hypnotic, as can be the roar of a rushing stream or waterfall. Such locations are often chosen for the tribal spiritual practice known as the vision quest. Psychoactive plants, herbs, vines and other botanical sources were also ingested to create other mental states, or used as forms of incense.

HINDUISM

The earliest religious documents from India, the Vedas, or 'wise sayings,' are ancient texts which give directions for every aspect of Hindu life. It was at the time of these writings that the caste system was established to help maintain the tradition. Originally, there were four castes – the priests (Brahmans) being the highest. Between 800 and 600 BC, the *Upanishads*, remarkable mystical and philosophical treatises written by various authors and which formed the later wisdom of India, abolished all the old gods. Only the great triad of Brahma, Vishnu and Shiva was maintained. And Brahma was the chief of the three. In Hindu philosophy, *Brahman* (also another name for Brahma) is the source of creation, and literally means 'to expand'. The concept of Brahman, in meditation, is used as an effective tool to expand consciousness.

A deeply religious Hindu is concerned exclusively with the inner life. The main focus of Hindu meditational practices, then, is to become aware of the ecstasy of the inner life. The Hindu use the word samadhi, which means 'ecstatic consciousness', and is interchangeable with the term nirvana, as their spiritual goal. As the *Dhammapada*, a collection of verses spoken by the Buddha, puts it: 'health is the greatest of gifts, contentedness the best of riches, trust the best of relationships. Nirvana is the highest happiness'.

Hindus striving toward a union with God obeyed a number of splintered disciplines that culminated into what we know as *yoga* (union). The term yoga, originally defined as a specific technique, inherited from physiological and spiritual concepts of which traces can be found in the Vedas. It acquired various diluted meanings in the course of history until, in the neo-Hinduism of modern times, it has come to describe any method for inducing mystical experience.

BUDDHISM

Siddhartha Gautama, the Buddha, was born in 563 BC in what is now Nepal. He founded Buddhism five centuries before the birth of Christianity. An entirely new branch of Hinduism, it had its source in the *Upanishads*, but rejected the Brahmanic doctrines, discounting the authority of the old Vedic laws and completely discarding the doctrines of caste, theology, priesthood and the ritual of the Brahmans. Moral living was more important to the Buddhists than ritualism. So in its purest form, Buddhism had no room for gods, priests, prayers, rituals or temples. Buddhism was in large measure a religion of reaction against Hindu perversions.

Buddha's teachings consisted of what were called Four Elementary Truths. The truths were the following:

(1) Life is dukkha (suffering).
(2) The cause of suffering is indulgence or desire.
(3) By ending desire we end suffering.
(4) The best way to end suffering is by application of wisdom and intelligence.

Buddhism also included an Eightfold Noble Path which, when followed, would bring about salvation. Buddha taught that nirvana was a state of mind, and therefore could best be reached by mental discipline.

One of the stages of the Eightfold Noble Path is 'right rapture', or earnest meditation, thought and contemplation on the deep mysteries of life. The principle is to follow your own convictions and conscience, releasing yourself from formal dogma. Eventually, though, not unusually, dogma crept into Buddhism, with the effect of Buddha becoming a god and nirvana a sort of heaven.

The basic meditative technique used in Buddhism was just to sit quietly and empty the mind. Buddhists felt that it was indeed possible to separate attention from thought. One way was to focus on the body and what was going on with it in the present moment.

Too much attention placed on thought blocks out reality: reality is the here and now, whereas thought is involved with either past or future events. Buddha taught that once the mind is empty, one will understand that nothingness is all the wisdom required in order to reach the state of ecstasy and total understanding.

Splinter sects arose – some imposing various forms of ritual practice – including, among others, Tibetan Buddhism, Taoism, and Zen.

TIBETAN BUDDHISM

The Tibetan Buddhists believe that the skills of concentration and insight are basic meditation techniques which are prerequisites for more advanced training.

Meditation is seen almost as a method of psychotherapy, with certain forms of meditation practised in controlled environments to 'treat' specific conditions.

They see the stage of nirvana, which is interpreted here as liberation from bondage – freedom from the endless cycle of reincarnations – as a prior stage to bodhisattvahood, in which the disciple returns to the world to help others to reach salvation.

The disciple becomes an *arhat* (enlightened being) when he reaches nirvana. To gain the superior state of being a bodhisattva, he must be motivated by love and compassion. In this way the disciple becomes a more perfect vehicle of compassion and can help others to attain a state of nirvana. To be a bodhisattva, according to the Dalai Lama, he must 'cleanse his mind of all impurities and remove the motives and inclinations that lead to them'. The Dalai Lama is the ruler and chief monk of Tibet. He is regarded as a reincarnation of all his predecessors and a manifestation of the national god of Tibet.

The Tibetan Buddhists employ the meditation technique of single-pointedness to help achieve nirvana, and believe that there are four steps in the process:

(1) Fixing the mind on the object of meditation and prolonging concentration on it.
(2) Allowing distractions to come and go, alternating with fixing the attention on the object of meditation.
(3) Feelings of joy and ecstasy arise, reinforcing the single-pointedness of the meditation – which enables total concentration.
(4) Total concentration comes with minimal effort.

The masters of the secret teachings of the Tibetan Buddhists say that truth learned from another is of no value: the only truth that is of value is that which we learn for ourselves. And as a the result master tells his neophytes to doubt everything, at least initially.

Doubt, even of things that had previously been taken for granted, should lead to enquiry in order to discover, for oneself, if they have a basis in reality. The term *lhag thong* is used, meaning 'the ability to see beyond the bounds limiting the vision of the cultivated mind'. To achieve lhag thong, one must put aside any preconceived ideas and look at everything as if for the first time. This is the way to knowledge.

TAOISM

The Chinese word *tao* simply means 'the way'. Lao Tze, born in China in 604 BC, was the founder of Taoism, a philosophical system which advocated a life of complete simplicity, naturalness, and non-interference with the course of natural events, in order to attain to a happy existence in harmony with Tao. Taoists consider themselves to be wanderers, in the sense that they live life as it comes to them, without clinging to any aspect of it, nor imposing any restrictions.

Early Taoism, like other serious meditative traditions, adhered to what we would consider today to be strict dietary rules, the primary one being to eat lightly. Grain, in the form of rice or wheat, tended to be the staple diet, with the addition of some vegetables, beancurd (tofu), and very little meat, poultry or fish. Berries, nuts, fruits and herbs gathered locally were also consumed.

Taoists do not attempt to provide concrete rules. Lao Tze wrote in the *Tao Tê Ching* over two and half millennia ago:

> *The way that can be told*
> *Is not the constant way;*
> *The name that can be named*
> *Is not the constant name.*

ZEN

Zen is a Japanese form of Buddhism introduced in Japan in the twelfth century, which is based on the practice of an intense and concentrated type of meditation, rather than a philosophy or a religious doctrine. The word zen is derived from the Sanskrit word *dhyana*, which means 'meditation'. The aim of Zen is 'no mind'. This means that a neutral stance is to be maintained at all times. It was felt that the mind should not dwell on any thing.

Zen meditation, or *zazen*, uses a wide variety of concentration techniques. For example, beginners are given breathing techniques. Other techniques involve sitting quietly, the objective being to achieve a heightened state of concentration, without any primary object to focus on: the aspirant is aware of what is going on around him but does not enter into any commentary within himself. He just sits and is aware.

A specifically Zen technique is known as the *koan*. Basically, the koan is a sort of puzzle that has no logical solution – the solution cannot be understood by language or thought.

One famous koan is: 'what is the sound of one hand clapping?' The aspirant is supposed to keep the koan constantly in his mind, no matter what he is doing. Theoretically, when the koan finally exhausts his logical thoughts, the aspirant's usual train of thinking is interrupted and he enters into a state of 'fixation', at which point, beyond logical thought, his koan reveals itself and he attains samadhi. In Zen terms, samadhi is a state of oneness in which the distinctions between things dissolve until, to the meditator, there is only a unified experience.

Satori (awakenings) is considered to follow samadhi. There are a variety of satori in Zen practice. The Zen practitioner is told to take no notice of any visions that he may have. Once satori is reached, it needs to be 'ripened' through further meditation, until it becomes part of the meditator's entire life. Details of everything that happens are perceived, but no evaluation is given; detachment is constantly maintained.

Much emphasis is placed on correct posture during Zen meditation. The meditator usually sits on a pillow on the floor, with legs crossed – most often in the lotus position. In this way the back is kept straight. The hands are folded in the lap with tips of thumbs touching. Eyes are kept open and lowered. Psychic powers are believed to arise naturally as the meditator reaches enlightenment – a process that usually takes many years to achieve. Hui Hai, an old Zen master, said: 'When things happen, make no response: keep your mind from dwelling on anything whatsoever'.

JUDEO-MYSTICISM

The roots of Jewish mysticism are found in the philosophies of the kabbalistic teachings. The *kabbala* is based on the Tree of Life, a cosmogram representing the passage of matter from its spiritual state into its final solid form. *Kether* represents the crown centre, and *malkuth* corresponds to the seat of matter.

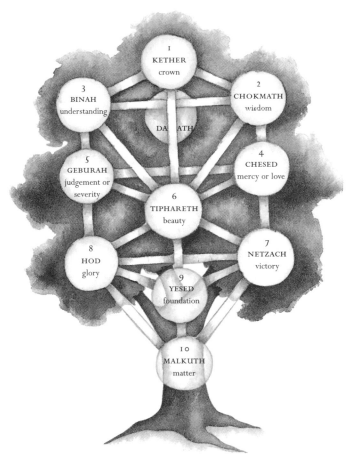

The ten sephiroth of the Tree of Life and the paths between them used in visualization journeys.

The kabbalists used the tree in their meditations. Their goal was to transmute the energy of the base of the tree (matter), through kether (crown), into its highest manifestation of the *ain soph* (God). The tree consists of ten *sephiroth*, a Hebrew term meaning holy emanations. Each branch of the tree symbolizes a development and attitude of deity as well as of man.

Among the meditative processes associated with this rich conceptualization is path-walking. The meditator is required to conduct visualized journeys along the paths of the tree, between the various sephiroth. The ultimate aim is, of course, to ensure that the meditator realizes his etheric and spiritual being and unites with God.

MYSTICAL CHRISTIANITY

In the fourth century, Christian monks spent much time in isolation and direct communion with God. In many ways, their practices were very similar to those of the Hindu and Buddhist faiths. For example the use of a rosary, a part of Christian devotion, is a reminder of the single-pointed meditation practised by early Hindu priests, and dates back to the Egyptian anchorites.

In its complete form, the rosary consists of a chain of 150 beads divided into tens (decades) which are separated by larger beads. The Sanskrit term *japa-mala*, which means 'muttering chaplet', describes the function of the rosary as a means of recording the number of prayers uttered. In the Catholic religion, the Lord's Prayer is recited on the larger beads, and the 'Hail, Mary' on the small beads. Each decade has a special theme for meditation including such events as the Annunciation, the Crucifixion and the Resurrection of Christ. The beads are used to keep track of the progress as the devotee recites each decade.

In 1960, Thomas Merton, an American poet and religious writer, observed that what is practised as prayer today in Christian churches is the survival of more intensive, contemplative practices. The monks living as hermits practised what would be described earlier as mantra meditation, involving the repetition of a very simple little prayer called the Jesus Prayer: 'Lord Jesus Christ Son of God have mercy on me, a sinner'. This is also known as the kyrie eleison, which would be repeated silently and continually throughout the day.

It was felt that this sort of meditation or prayer would lead the seeker towards the highest human perfection.

These practices were widespread in both Eastern Orthodox and Roman Catholic contemplative traditions. Contemplation entails concentrating the mind – one-pointedness – on its own, deepest aspects, in order to connect with God.

In all traditional religions, prayer is commonly used. However, in most of these religions it is not given in its mantric form; consequently no shift of consciousness occurs. When praying aloud intensively, outward chatter is reduced, creating a monotonous but calming atmosphere – as is always the case when ritual words are repeated over and over.

Rituals in a church environment often provide meditational aids, such as music or the sound of bells ringing, a waft of incense, the flicker of a votive candle, and the adoption of a particular praying posture.

SUFISM

Sufism, the name given to the mystical aspect of the Islamic religion, originated in the seventh century. The word *sufi* is derived from the Arabic for 'wool', and was commonly used to describe the wool clothing worn by the early followers of this philosophy, who copied the dress of Christian monks of that time.

The main meditation technique used by the Sufis is called *zikr*, meaning 'remembrance'. Mantra is part of this practice. The recitation of the mantra 'la illaha illa 'lla' hu' (which means 'there is no God but God') produces a state of meditative consciousness. While this mantra is being recited, some Sufi sects simultaneously rotate their head and neck in a prescribed circular motion, which helps to produce an even higher state of ecstasy.

The most popularly known Sufi meditative technique is dancing. One form of dance is a specific spinning technique (giving us the image of the 'whirling dervish'). As in yoga, the entire body is used to reach a meditative state. The use of such a method helps to release energies which are located in the spinal cord. Eastern tradition believes that the release of these energies helps us to reach the meditative state.

Music is another important technique used by the Sufis to reach a higher state of consciousness. The tonal quality, in particular, helps in the meditative process. Sufis consider that certain notes activate areas in our physical being which help us to achieve higher states. For example, the high 'E' sound they use is thought to activate the so-called third eye centre, which is supposed to affect a person's ability to achieve a higher state of vision.

YOGA

Yoga, a Hindu system of philosophy, is made up of teachings which have come down through centuries of thought, investigation, experiment and experience. These teachings were passed on from teacher to pupil, and gradually, a definite yogic science evolved, in which seven systems can be discerned. According to yogic teaching, the choice of which system to follow is subject to individual temperament: each leads to the same end – unfoldment, development and growth. The seven yogic systems are:

Hatha yoga

Probably the most popular Eastern tradition that the West has embraced is hatha yoga. In the United States, many people practise its exercises mainly because it produces physical results not found in any other system. *Hatha yoga* – meaning force in Sanskrit – is concerned with the physical body and its development: it is said to consciously fill it with life force.

There are over eighty *asanas* (body postures) in

hatha yoga, the majority of which are only taught to the highest spiritual aspirants. The main purpose of achieving these postures is to gain the correct bodily poise which will enable the mind to attain a contemplative state.

Tantra yoga

This is said to be a refinement of earlier shamanic practices, and defines a type of yoga applied to the stilling of the mind. Tantric yoga concerns itself with transforming the base level energy into the higher levels of consciousness. According to the Tantric system, consciousness is altered by the awakening and directing of a normally dormant psychic force, known as kundalini.

Kundalini is considered to be a reserve of spiritual power consisting of two energies, *ida* and *pingala*. It can supposedly be roused from its normal location at the base of the spine, and ascend a channel within the spinal cord. When all the necessary practices are performed to start it moving, ida and pingala rise up the spine separately – pingala on the right side and ida on the left – until they reach the sixth chakra *(ajna)* which is located between the eyebrows. At this point ida and pingala cross over each other, providing the opportunity for breakthrough to the next highest level, or seventh chakra *(sahasrana)*, located at the top or crown of the head, and is the doorway to cosmic consciousness.

The practice of maithuna, which is a tantric technique, concerns itself with transforming the base chakra level energy into the higher levels of consciousness and involves intercourse. Sexual energy is used because it is the quickest way to awaken kundalini. Today, this energy has been shown scientifically to be an electrical impulse which can be triggered by the human mind in certain stages of meditation.

Mantra yoga

This yogic system employs sound vibration to produce an effect on the mind, the body, and the emotions. The term 'mantra yoga' represents continuous repetition of a sound vibration given by the teacher to students to affect a particular part of their body – or more accurately, one of their chakras.

Sounds produced by a mantra include those that are not normally audible. Practitioners consider a mantra to be a projection of cosmic sound, and that the entire world is framed in mantra equations. The yogis were aware of ultrasonic sound vibrations which have, only relatively recently, been rediscovered by modern science. The highest mantra is the word 'aum' (pronounced 'ohm'). Its expression represents the presence of the Creator.

In meditation, the vocal sound of a mantra is ultimately internalized, to become a mental, soundless resonance, acting as a kind of 'waveguide' for the meditator's consciousness as it reaches for higher levels.

Bhakta yoga

This system follows the path of the heart – with which most yoga students have an affinity. Bhakta can be applied to any branch of yoga. There is no particular style or practice specific to it but a mantra that opens the heart centre is used. Bhakta is found in every religion: it corresponds to the yearning for a union with God. Consequently, it can open the heart to love on every level.

Karma yoga

This is a yoga of action — deeds applied to our daily life. Karma is, basically, the law of cause and effect: 'Cast your bread upon the waters and it shall return'. Karma yoga affects the moral attitudes in everyday life. Be careful of what you think about as it will most likely manifest! The Karma yogi feels that we build our future in everyday action. The seeds we plant can either grow into flowers or weeds.

Jnana yoga

This system attracts intellectuals. They follow a course of continual inquiry and seek the answer to the constant 'why?' Truth is continually questioned. This yoga could be called 'the union with wisdom'.

Raja yoga

This term signifies 'kingly'. Raja yoga works towards mastery of the inner self, and depends on independence. Raja has been described as the synthesis of three yogas — bhakta, karma and jnana. In a way, it is a summary of all the other types of yoga. To practise raja one must follow hatha yoga: hatha yoga emphasizes the practical, raja yoga emphasizes the superior. The perfecting of the body by hatha ultimately releases the mental freedom necessary for raja.

Siddha yoga

In the 1960s, Swami Muktananda taught a modern form of yoga in the United States, which he called siddha yoga. This system incorporates traditional practices such as asana (body postures), pramayam (practice of right breathing) and chanting.

A strong guru-disciple relationship is required, and the practice can take up to twelve years. During the practice, the guru grants the devotee shaktipat diksha (a direct and instantaneous transcendental experience) — the guru is supposed to be able to directly arouse the normally dormant psychic energy in a devotee.

The siddha yoga method of meditation is said to unveil awareness of the self — different from the normal conscious state in which the awareness is externally directed. To achieve this, techniques are used to mask the distractions of the outer world, in the same way as a Faraday cage is used to block off electromagnetic waves.

TRANSCENDENTAL MEDITATION

Transcendental meditation, or TM, was among the first techniques that brought the practice of meditation into a twentieth-century context. This practice has its roots in Hindu mantra meditation, and is based on the teachings of the eighth-century Indian religious philosopher, Sankaracharya. The object of these teachings is to attain the union of the seeker's mind with infinite consciousness.

Maharishi Mahesh first started teaching transcendental deep meditation in India. In 1958, he started to teach in various countries, before arriving in California in 1959. From there, his teaching spread across the United States to New York, and onward into Europe. This process was greatly aided by the popularity given the TM movement by the Beatles and other pop luminaries of the 1960s. It is said that the Beatles actually made use of some of the mantric rhythms they learned in TM for their music. By 1975, there were almost 10,000 trained teachers of TM. And because this technique was particularly embraced by the young, the Society that had been founded by Maharishi became the Students' International Meditation Society.

As with all meditation, the basic principle of TM is to reduce mental activity, allowing subtler levels of the mind to enter consciousness. The idea is to turn the attention away from the outer world of sensory experience, towards the subtler, inner levels of the mind – but without actually thinking about it. TM uses mantras as meditational aids for carrying the attention to subtler levels of the mind, to reach the source of the thought.

As its influence and resources grew, TM instigated and sponsored some interesting scientific research into mind/body interactions, particularly as exemplified in the practice of meditation. Notably, they encouraged research into the effects of meditation on psychosomatic characteristics of stress disorders.

Some TM techniques have now passed into mainstream usage in both medical and corporate contexts. Despite this contribution by TM, it has now to some extent passed its peak of popularity and one hears about it primarily in terms of sensational reports concerning supposed levitation said to occur in particular TM states. The actual status of such reported phenomena is still subject to neutral research.

MEDITATION IN THE WESTERN WORLD

Modern adaptations of established meditative techniques began in earnest in Western societies during the 1960s. This period coincided with the worldwide spread of Tibetan Buddhism as a result of the Chinese invasion of Tibet, which also led to the establishment of several Western Buddhist orders.

Westerners then increasingly came into physical contact with Eastern spiritual teachers, either by journeying to India and elsewhere to sit at their feet, or as a result of such gurus visiting the West. A new traffic in spiritual ideas and practices was therefore set up, and it began to influence Western society on a hitherto unprecedented scale.

The Beat poets of the 1950s, such as Jack Kerouac, Allen Ginsberg and Lawrence

Ferlinghetti, for example, had been he first to generate an interest in Zen Buddhism. Western youth, feeling spiritually disenfranchised, were looking for new ways to religious truths. They rejected most of the organized concepts of religion and philosophy and sought more than rote-belief systems. This ultimately led to the rediscovery of the esoteric and spiritual concepts of the East – what the great English writer, Aldous Huxley, called the 'Perennial Philosophy'.

Such transplantation of traditions was not new. The Greek Plotinus (AD 205-270) brought back philosophies and ideas from Persia and India which greatly influenced the Christian mystics of his time. And in the nineteenth century, Eastern traditions found their way into the writing of Emerson and Thoreau, and the poetry of Walt Whitman.

Eventually, it was in the field of psychology, and specifically transpersonal psychology – dealing with mental experiences of a transcendental nature – that the impact of Eastern religions and philosophy on Western culture had its greatest impact and far-reaching influence.

William James was probably the first American psychologist to include Eastern ideas in his thinking. In 1893, he met Swami Vivekananda at the First World Congress of Religions, and wrote the classic, *Varieties of Religious Experience*, which explores the psychological elements of religion.

But it was Alan Watts, the San Francisco-based English writer on Eastern religions and philosophy, who was the most influential in bringing Eastern teachings to the awareness of Western psychologists. Watts lectured widely, and wrote a series of books comparing Eastern philosophy to Western psychotherapy, convinced that both practices were equally concerned with changing people's feelings about themselves and those around them, and ultimately about nature.

More recently, Charles Tart, Professor of Psychology at the University of California, compared the Buddhist term *samsara* (a state of consciousness described as illusion, but considered to be our normal state of consciousness) with terms used in Western psychology. He warns ,however, that while Eastern thought has a great deal to teach Western culture, it is important to adapt some of its aspects to our Western society rather than import it wholesale.

Yet what has brought meditation into general awareness in the West is not so much the various adaptations of Eastern philosophy to Western psychology. It is, above all, a growing sense of the impoverishment of the soul within an increasingly industrialized, mechanistic and dehumanizing society. This is leading people to seek new and effective answers to their spiritual yearnings. And meditation is undoubtedly one of them.

FURTHER READING

Ackerman, Diane. *A Natural History of the Senses*. New York: Vintage, 1990

Arberry, A. J. *Sufism – an Account of the Mystics of Islam*. London: Allen and Unwin Paperbacks, 1979. US dist: Paul & Co. Pubs, Consortium

Benson, H. *The Relaxation Response*. New York: Avon, 1976

Birren, Faber. *Color & Human Response*. New York: Van Nostrand Reinhold Company, 1978

———. *Color*. New York: Citadel Press, 1963

———. *Principles of Color*. Atglen, PA: Schiffer Publishing, 1987

———. *Psychology and Color Therapy*. New York: The Citadel Press, 1950

Blofeld, John. *Gateway to Wisdom*. Austin, TX: Mandala Books, 1980

Cade, C. Maxwell, and Nona Coxhead. *The Awakened Mind*. Rockport, MA: Element Books, 1979

Carrington, Patricia. PhD. *Freedom in Meditation*. New York: Anchor Press-Doubleday, 1977

Cavendish, Richard. *Encyclopedia of the Unexplained*. New York: Routledge & Kegan Paul, 1974

Chaitow, Leon. *Clear Body Clear Mind*. London: Allen and Unwin Paperbacks, 1990

Ch'gyam, Ngakpa. *Rainbow of Liberated Energy*. Rockport, MA: Element Books, 1986

Clark, Linda. *The Ancient Art of Color Therapy*. New York: Pocket Books, 1975

Coleman, Daniel. *The Meditative Mind*. Bodega Bay, CA: Crucible, 1988

Cooper, J. C. *An Illustrated Encyclopaedia of Traditional Symbols*. London: Thames & Hudson, 1978

Deikman, Arthur J. *The Observing Self*. Boston, MA: Beacon Press, 1982

Devereux, Charla. *The Aromatherapy Kit*. Boston, MA: Charles E. Tuttle Co., Inc., 1993

———. *The Perfume Kit*. New York: Macmillan, 1996

Dossey, Larry. MD. *Healing Words*. San Fransisco: Harper SF, 1995

Gibson, Walter. *The Key to Yoga*. East Brunswick, NJ: Bell Publishing Co, 1958

Gilbert, R. A. *The Elements of Mysticism*. Rockport, MA: Element Books, 1991

Gimbel, Theo, and Pauline Wills. *16 Steps to Health and Energy*. Saint Paul, MN: Llewellyn Publications, 1992

Hardon, John A. *Religions of the World*. New York: Image Books, 1968

Happold, F. C. *Mysticism*. New York: Viking Penguin, 1991

Heline, Corinne. *Healing and Regeneration through Color*. Marina del Ray, CA: DeVorss Press, 1983

Humphrey, Naomi. *Meditation the Inner Way*. San Diego, CA: Aquarian Press, 1987

Jung, C. G. *Modern Man in Search of a Soul*. New York: Harvest Books, 1933

Katz, Richard. *Boiling Energy*. Cambridge, MA: Harvard University Press, 1982

Khan, Pir Vilayat Inayat. *Towards the One*. New York, Harper Collins, 1974

Khanna, Madhu. *Yantra*. London: Thames & Hudson, 1994

Lings, Martin. *What is Sufism?* Santa Rosa, CA: Atrium Publications, 1995

Lüscher, Dr Max. *Color Test*. New York: Washington Square Press, 1969

Puharich, Andrija. *Beyond Telepathy*. London:

Pan Books Ltd, 1962

Radhakrishnan, S. *Eastern Religions and Western Thought*. New York: Oxford University Press, 1969 (1939)

Reber, Arthur S. *Dictionary of Psychology*. New York: Penguin Books, 1985

Renou, Louis. *The Nature of Hinduism*. New York: Walker and Co., 1962

Rinpoche, Sogyal. *Meditation*. San Francisco, CA: Harper SF, 1994

Roney-Dougal, Serena. *Where Science and Magic Meet*. Rockport, MA: Element Books, 1991

Russell, Peter. *The TM Technique*. New York: Arkana, 1978

———. *The Brain Book*. New York: NAL Dutton, 1984

Rycroft, Charles. *Dictionary of Psychoanalysis*. London: Penguin Books Ltd, 1995

Seward, Barbara. *The Symbolic Rose*. Woodstock, CT: Spring Publications Inc., 1989

Smith, Huston. *The Religions of Man*. New York: Harper & Row, 1958

Swami, Rama, R. Ballentine, and A. Hymes. *Science of Breath*. Honesdale, PA: Himalayan International Institute, 1979

Tomkins, P., and C. Bird. *The Secret Life of Plants*. New York: Avon, 1974

Tucci, Giuseppe. *The Theory and Practice of the Mandala*. York Beach, ME: Samuel Weiser, 1973

Tulku, Rarthang. *Reflections of Mind*. Berkeley, CA: Dharma Publishing, 1975

von Goethe, Johann Wolfgang. *Theory of Colours*. Cambridge, MA: The M.I.T. Press, 1970 (1840)

Weil, Andrew. MD. *Spontaneous Healing*. New York: Fawcett Columbine, 1995

INDEX

Page numbers in *italics* refer to illustrations

AUTHOR'S ACKNOWLEDGEMENTS

The study and practice of meditation started seriously for me in 1977, when I met Fran Stockel. At that time, Fran held a meditation group once a week and I became part of it. Meditation has been a part of my life since then – in addition to incorporating meditation in my daily routine, I have helped set up a number of meditation groups over the years.

When I asked Fran to contribute to this book, her initial reaction was one of horror. She was an artist by trade and her tool was the paint brush, not the pen. But in the end, as this kit confirms, she consented to write her thoughts on the four meditation themes, and offered advice and thoughts for some of the other sections. Incidentally, the concept of theme meditation presented in this kit originated in a powerful dream.

Numerous other people have played a part in shaping my views and knowledge of meditation. Among them I would particularly like to thank: Maria McKenna, Mary Jane Ridder, Marcy Losapio, Dorothy Odle, Shirley Cohen, Eva Graf, Eugene Graf, Sheila Withus, Ian Cooke, Tom Henderson-Smith, Eileen Hertzberg and Sue Robinson, and of course, my husband Paul.

Both Fran and I are indebted to the teachings of Pir Vilayat Inyat Khan who so greatly influenced Fran's spiritual path and also touched upon my own.

We also want to thank all the staff at Eddison Sadd who have helped us in producing this kit, and particularly Ian Jackson.

EDDISON•SADD EDITIONS

Project Editor	Cecilia Walters
Editorial Assistance	Pat Pierce
Indexer	Dorothy Frame
Art Director	Elaine Partington
Senior Art Editor	Sarah Howerd
Assistant Designer	Shefton Somersall-Weekes
Illustrator	Rosamund Fowler
Production	Hazel Kirkman and Charles James

Special thanks for the production of THE MEDITATION TAPE to Darren, Alex, Lee and Natalie at EMR, and to Tim Cummins for the mantras.

The sound of bees on THE MEDITATION TAPE is copyright the BBC Natural History Sound Library, and is reproduced by kind permission.

With thanks to Rosamund Fowler for her commitment to the project.

PICTURE CREDITS
Photograph on page 27 by Stephen Marwood. The images on the meditation cards and on pages 34 and 35, and throughout the book, are copyright Planet Earth Pictures (Rose: Rosemary Calvert, Waterfall: William Smithey, Skyscape: Jean-Paul Nacivet, Lightning: T.A. Wiewandt).